A LIFE

A LIFE

A PLAY BY

HUGH LEONARD

ATHENEUM
NEW YORK

CAUTION: Professionals and amateurs are hereby warned that *A Life,* being fully protected under the Copyright Laws of the United States of America, the British Empire, including the Dominion of Canada, and all other countries of the Berne and Universal Copyright Conventions, is subject to royalty. All rights, including professional, amateur, motion picture, recitation, lecturing, public reading, radio and television broadcasting, and the rights of translation into foreign languages, are strictly reserved. Permission for any use must be secured in writing from the author's agent, Gilbert Parker, William Morris Agency, 1350 Avenue of the Americas, New York, New York 10019, except for amateur and stock acting rights, which are controlled exclusively by Samuel French, Inc., 25 W. 45th Street, New York, New York, 10036. Permission must be secured in writing from Samuel French, Inc., before any such performance may be scheduled.

An amateur acting edition has been published by SAMUEL FRENCH, INC., which edition contains complete stage directions.

Photographs by Ed Ellis

Copyright © 1980 by Hugh Leonard
All rights reserved
Published simultaneously in Canada by McClelland and Stewart Ltd.
Printed in the United States of America

A Life opened in New York on November 2, 1980 at the Morosco Theatre. It was produced by Lester Osterman, Richard Horner, Hinks Shimberg and Freydberg-Cutler-Diamond Productions. Associate Producer was Lynne Stuart. Scenery and Costumes were by Robert Fletcher. The lighting was designed by Marc B. Weiss. The cast was as follows:

DRUMM	Roy Dotrice
DOLLY	Helen Stenborg
MARY	Aideen O'Kelly
MIBS	Lauren Thompson
DESMOND	Adam Redfield
LAR	David Ferry
KEARNS	Pat Hingle
DOROTHY	Dana Delany

A LIFE

ACT ONE

Darkness. Then lights come up on a stone bandstand at Stage Centre. It is octagonal in shape, and although the roof is long gone, the supporting pillars of curved Victorian iron remain. A short flight of stone steps leads down to Stage level. The Stage areas to Left and Right of the bandstand are in darkness.
DRUMM *is standing on the bandstand.* HE *is wearing a fawn-coloured raincoat.* HE *refreshes his memory by glancing at his notes, then puts them away.* HE *addresses an unseen audience.*

DRUMM: To conclude. I have chosen to terminate today's walk in this park, which is remarkable for its views of sea and mountains, such as may have inspired Bernard Shaw's observation that whereas Ireland's men are temporal, her hills are eternal. Any child familiar with the rudiments of geology could have told him otherwise, but then even Shaw was not immune to his countrymen's passion for inexactitude. These few acres have more than a scenic claim on our attention. This hillside is all that remains of what was called the Commons of Dalkey. Where the town—I speak in the Catholic sense; the Protestants call it a village—where it now stands there was once only gorseland and furze, moorland and wretched cabins. The coming of the railway in 1834 turned the wilderness into a place of habitation for the well-to-do, who were closely followed by tradespeople and members of the middle classes who knew their place and on that account lost no time in leaving it. The town evolved, grew and procreated, as our presence in it bears witness. Its population is four thousand seven hundred, which

figure can by simple division be broken down into nearly six hundred persons per public house. It was known to antiquity as the Town of the Seven Castles, of which the surviving two are vermin-infested, one being in ruins and the other the town hall. (*A thin smile, which disappears when there is no response to his joke*) The climate is temperate, the birthrate relentless and the mortal—(HE *hesitates*)—the mortality rate is consistent with the national average. I see that some of you become restive. (HE *looks at his watch*) And, coincidentally, the licensing laws are about to be in our favour. I thank you for your attention. The next of the conducted walks so ingeniously entitled "Dalkey Discovered" will take place four weeks from today, on Sunday, June sixteenth. Your guide will be Mrs. Rachel Fogarty. Good day.
(*There is a thin spatter of applause, which suggests that his audience has been a thin one.* HE *watches them leave, then takes a tube of milk of magnesia tablets from his pocket and puts one in his mouth.* HE *sits on the steps of the bandstand and takes out a packet of Sweet Afton. With the cigarette halfway to his lips,* HE *sits absolutely still as if a realisation had suddenly come to him. A* WOMAN *appears.* SHE *is his wife,* DOLLY, *aged sixty*)

DOLLY (*Approaching*): Woo-ee! Dezzie!
  (DRUMM'S *only reaction is to complete the business of lighting his cigarette*)
DOLLY (*Continued*): I came to meet you.
DRUMM (*Not pleased*): Did you?
DOLLY: I climbed over the very tiptop and down the rocks. Amn't I great? (*Catching her breath*) Whoo . . . It's so steep, I thought to myself, God send I don't burst into a run and can't stop.
DRUMM: It would have enlivened my lecture.
DOLLY: I saw you from the top, talking sixteen to the dozen, only I couldn't hear and I didn't want to come down and make you nervous, so I waited. Was it a nice walk, what way did you go, what did you say to them?
DRUMM: You are the only woman I know who can talk while breathless.

DOLLY: I was dying to hear. Were they thrilled to bits?
DRUMM: They managed not to disintegrate. I spoke well. I think I did. It's unimportant.
(DOLLY *has a natural gaiety, under which is a terror of his displeasure.* SHE *seizes at any opportunity of staying in his good graces*)
DOLLY: Do you hear him! Where'd you walk them to?
DRUMM: To here.
DOLLY: You're mean. No, tell us.
DRUMM (*With a sigh, as if to say "If I must"*): Along the Metals by the old Atmospheric Railway, around the hill, along the Green Road to the broken cross and from there to the old semaphore station, which, thanks to my sense of smell, I kept them from entering. Then to Torca Cottage, and here by way of the Cat's Ladder and the Ramparts.
DOLLY: Such a distance.
DRUMM (*With satisfaction*): I think I may say that I lost one or two of them en route.
DOLLY: And you made a lovely speech.
DRUMM: Not a speech: I gave a talk.
DOLLY: And it's not everyone they ask. They're most particular.
(HE *looks at her coldly*)
DOLLY (*Continued*): And if they didn't ask you itself, a pity about them. What are they, only from the town.
DRUMM: Why did you come here?
DOLLY: To meet you.
DRUMM: I'm aware of that. I asked why.
DOLLY: I got tired of the four walls for company. (*Aware that* HE *is looking at her*) The sun was splitting the trees out. You told me where you'd be finishing up, and I said why don't I give myself an outing and the pair of us can walk home.
DRUMM: So you went crawling through the gorse like a decrepit sheep.
(SHE *has no ready answer. Pause*)
DOLLY: You put me in mind of an old statue.
DRUMM: What?

DOLLY: When I was coming down. You were sitting with the cigarette halfway to your mouth and not a jig out of you. No more life than an old statue.
DRUMM: I was admiring the view.
DOLLY: No, you weren't. Like a statue by that French artist.
DRUMM: Not artist. Sculptor.
DOLLY: Mm, by him . . . what's-his-name.
DRUMM (*Deliberately*): Renoir.
DOLLY: Mm. (*A pause*) And I'm not a sheep, Dezzie.
DRUMM: Quite so.
DOLLY: Or decrepit, either.
DRUMM: To be sure.
DOLLY: I know it's only your way and you mean nothing by it, but other people don't know that, and it's not very—
DRUMM: Could we have done?
DOLLY: —very gentlemanly.
(HE *looks at the view as if* SHE *were not there*)
DOLLY (*Continued*): Are you not going to tell me what Ben said?
DRUMM: Who?
DOLLY: Ben Mulhall. I know you were in with him because I met Maddie Dowling in the chapel yard and she said she saw you coming out of his front gate.
DRUMM: So that's why.
DOLLY: Why what?
(HE *does not answer: it is as if a reply would be beneath contempt*)
DOLLY (*Continued*): I thought maybe he'd had news for you.
DRUMM (*Affirmative*): Mm.
DOLLY: Had he?
DRUMM: We met in the street. I asked him if he had had the results of the X rays. He took me into his surgery; I think that being in it reassures him that he's a doctor. He gave me one of those looks of his, redolent of the cemetery, and said that I should buy day returns from now on instead of season tickets.
DOLLY: Oh, Dezzie . . .
DRUMM (*Annoyed*): He was being fatuous. Do you think

he'd make jokes in the face of having his practice diminished by another patient? After he had used up his small reservoir of wit, he condescended to get to the point. My own diagnosis was correct: I have a duodenal ulcer. He is to give me a diet sheet and a prescription, and he said that I am to watch myself. I told him that my name was Drumm, not Narcissus. Of course it was lost on him too.

DOLLY: You won't have to go into—I mean, to be—

DRUMM: Certainly not. Only a fool donates his body to science *before* death. Mulhall said that I am to drink milk instead of tea or coffee. Then senility overcame him and he began to babble about my giving up whiskey as well. An ulcer: one lives with it, but at least one lives.

(DOLLY *turns her head away and searches in her bag for a handkerchief*)

DRUMM (*Continued*): Now what?

DOLLY: Nothing.

DRUMM: Not tears.

DOLLY: I'm grand.

DRUMM: Are you so disappointed?

DOLLY: Over what? (*Taking his meaning, reproachfully*) I'm relieved.

DRUMM: Oh, yes?

DOLLY: That's a terrible thing to—

DRUMM: Lower your voice.

DOLLY: Making out I was disapp—

DRUMM: This is a public place. You are incapable of recognising a joke when you hear it.

DOLLY: It wasn't a—

(HE *silences her with a look*)

DOLLY (*Continued*): I was worried sick.

DRUMM: I didn't notice.

DOLLY: I wasn't going to let on to you, was I? But let's face it, Dezzie, we're not youngsters, and when you get to be our age—

DRUMM: Don't bracket our ages.

DOLLY: It's just the sort of thing that happens when you think at long last you're grand and clear and have the chance to enjoy life. Do you know what I said? I said: Ah, no, God, not now, not when he'll be finished with the office in August and we can have our holiday and a rest and get the little car and—

(SHE *stops, dismayed that* SHE *has said more than* SHE *ought. Pause.* HE *waits until* SHE *tries to disentangle herself*)

DOLLY (*Continued*): I mean—
DRUMM: What little car?
DOLLY: If you owned up to it, you were as worried as I was.
DRUMM: You said a car.
DOLLY: When?

(*As* HE *draws in his breath; deprecatingly*)

DOLLY (*Continued*): A small one.
DRUMM: Do you mean a motorcar?
DOLLY: They're all the go.
DRUMM: All the . . . ?

(SHE *giggles nervously at the accidental pun*)

DOLLY: Amn't I a panic.
DRUMM: What new foolishness is this?
DOLLY: We could afford it. You'll have your lump sum. (*Weakly*) It'd be nice.
DRUMM: How long has this been fermenting inside that brain of yours? A car. To be driven by whom, may I ask?
DOLLY: You could go for lessons.
DRUMM: You think so?
DOLLY: An ulcer wouldn't hinder you.
DRUMM: I daresay.
DOLLY: The Moroneys bought themselves one, and he gets blackouts.
DRUMM: And have you yet decided where we'll go in it, in this small car?
DOLLY: For . . . drives.
DRUMM (*Without intonation*): Drives.
DOLLY: And we could visit people. Friends.
DRUMM: Such as whom?
DOLLY (*Vaguely*): You know.

DRUMM: Friends, you said. Who?
DOLLY: New friends.
(HE *decides that* HE *has heard enough.* HE *brushes down his coat and buttons it*)
DOLLY (*Continued*): Don't be cross, Dezzie. I thought it'd be an interest for you.
DRUMM: I'm not at all cross, and it is of no interest either to me or for me. You take too much on yourself. Without consulting me, you sit weaving your little webs, letting your imagination run riot. And then, when I speak to you with the voice of reason, you come crashing to earth. You do yourself no kindness at all. Look here: don't you think there are enough fools and blackguards walking about on two legs without my having to contend with those in motorcars as well? Driving lessons, indeed.
DOLLY: If you don't want to learn, maybe I could.
DRUMM (*Not unkindly*): Have sense. The entire population would take to the fields. (HE *looks at his watch*) A quarter to. Go, now: off home with you.
DOLLY: I thought the pair of us could—
DRUMM: —walk home. You said. I have a call to make.
DOLLY: Where?
(HE *gives her one of his looks, as if* SHE *should know better by now than to pry*)
DOLLY (*Continued*): I mean, I put the leg of lamb on for two o'clock. You won't be late?
DRUMM: Have I ever been late?
DOLLY: No, Dezzie.
DRUMM: No, never. Off you go, then.
DOLLY: Well, don't be—
(SHE *checks herself and sets off.* HE *watches until* SHE *is out of sight, then goes towards the area at Stage Right, perhaps disappearing from view for a moment.*
Lights come up at Stage Right on the living room of a small red-bricked Edwardian house of the kind with a pocket-handkerchief garden in front. The room is neat and homely. It is newly decorated, and some of the furniture—perhaps the three-piece suite—is new as well.

There is a television set and an electric fire with imitation logs. MARY KEARNS *comes in.* SHE *is of an age with* DOLLY. SHE *is followed by* DRUMM)

MARY: What is it they say? The dead arose and appeared to many. Come in.

DRUMM: If you're sure I'm welcome.

MARY: That's the last thing I'm sure of.

(HE *stops in his tracks, affronted*)

MARY (*Continued*): (*Confused*) I dunno whether you are or not.

DRUMM: If you'd prefer I hadn't called . . .

MARY: I'll tell you that when I hear what brought you. (*Looking at him*) The same old face on you. A body daren't look crossways at you.

DRUMM: You're in an aggressive mood.

MARY: I'm surprised, do you mind?

DRUMM (*Reasonably*): I daresay it would be surprising if you weren't. Perhaps this isn't convenient.

MARY: Ah, don't be such a dry stick.

DRUMM: I could call another time.

MARY: Aye, in another six years. Will you take that raincoat off you and sit. Wrapped up like an old mummy in the month of May.

DRUMM: A prudent man waits until June.

MARY: And one day you ought to go demented and buy yourself a new one. Give it me.

DRUMM (*Removing his coat*): Is he in?

MARY: Is who in?

DRUMM: Your husband.

MARY: In or out, he has a name.

DRUMM: Yes. Is he here?

(SHE *snatches the coat and bunches up her fist in exasperation, shoving it up to his face*)

MARY: I'll do it yet, you see if I don't. He's at the—(*Taking care to mention the name*) Lar is at Finnegan's, having his pint.

DRUMM (*Smiling sceptically*): Pint, singular.

(SHE *does not deign to answer, but puts his coat away. We notice for the first time that* SHE *limps slightly*)

DRUMM (*Continued*): Are you well?

MARY: The way you see me.

DRUMM: Fully recovered, I meant. The accident.

MARY: You're behind the times. I'm over that this long while.

DRUMM: I was concerned.

MARY: I know; I got your letter. I was surprised there wasn't a "Your obedient servant" at the end of it. (*Regretting this*) And you sent Dolly to see me. It was nice of you.

DRUMM (*Reasonably*): You'd been injured.

MARY: I do often say to Lar, I was such a good patient they put a barometer inside my leg for a present. It gives me the weather forecast.

DRUMM: The limp is hardly noticeable. Does it trouble you?

MARY: Only when people mention it.

DRUMM: You look very well indeed. Hardly a day older.

MARY: Since when? Yesterday?

DRUMM: I mean, since we—

MARY: You go past me every day in the town. I might as well be a midge in the air or a pane of glass a body'd look through. If you see me in time, you go across the street, and if you don't, you put that face on you as if there was a dead dog in the road. Making a show of yourself and of me as well.

DRUMM: We weren't on speaking terms.

MARY: And don't I know it!

DRUMM: I am not a hypocrite. I will not affect a pretence of goodwill simply for the benefit of every prying cornerboy and twitching lace curtain in the street.

MARY: A nod wouldn't have killed you.

DRUMM: You'd prefer me to be dishonest?

MARY: Be whatever you like. You're a bitter old pill, and you always will be.

DRUMM (*Smiling tolerantly*): I have never yet met the member of your sex who didn't prefer common abuse to common sense.

MARY: Did you come in here to vex me?
DRUMM: No. No, I did not, and your point is well taken. Whatever bitterness has been between us is in the past.
MARY (*Ominously*): It's where?
DRUMM: I thought is was time we were friends again.
MARY: Is that what brung you?
DRUMM (*Gently*): Brought me.
MARY: Brought you.
DRUMM: At our age, there aren't so many days left that one can afford to squander them in quarrels.
MARY: Life's too short.
DRUMM: Exactly.
MARY: That's the bee in your bonnet, is it? And so you walk in here, calm as you like after six years, expecting the welcome mat and to be offered rashers and eggs.
(HE *makes no reply*)
MARY (*Continued*): Do you want a cup of tea?
DRUMM: No, thank you.
MARY: There's a drop of whiskey.
DRUMM (*Considering*): Ah. Well, in that case I won't give offence, as they say, with a refusal.
(SHE *goes to the sideboard*)
DRUMM (*Continued*): The merest tincture. It'll sharpen the appetite. Dolly is doing us a leg of lamb.
MARY: How is she?
DRUMM: Unchanged.
MARY: This is a sudden notion of yours.
DRUMM: Pardon me?
MARY: To make up.
DRUMM: I had some news this morning to do with health. Good news. (*As* SHE *glances at him*) I wasn't ill, but there was the possibility. A cloud threatening the autumn day.
MARY: And it's gone now?
DRUMM: A passing shower.
MARY: So you feel full of yourself.
DRUMM: That, too, perhaps. But it brought it home to me that one's time is finite. If instead of cracking his execra-

ble jokes Ben Mulhall had offered me that whiskey and if his eyes had avoided mine—

MARY: What was it that ailed you?

DRUMM: Tummy trouble. And if these antennae and these (HE *gestures towards his eyes and ears*) had detected a verdict of another kind, well, I would have lived to reg— (HE *amends, smiling*) I would have regretted those six years.

MARY: Will you pour this? I never know how much. (SHE *gives him the bottle and a glass*) Six years? Did you ever add up all the time we haven't been talking since I knew you? How many days out of the forty? You're an Irish summer of a man: sunny skies one day and rain the next. For a week or maybe a month you'd be the height of company: you'd make a cat laugh; next thing, there's a face on you like a plateful of mortal sins, and you're off out that door as if there was a curtain rod stuck up you. You can get on with no one: a cup of cold water would disagree with you.

DRUMM: You say that, but in your heart you know that I am the most reasonable man in this town.

MARY: Drink your drink.

DRUMM: As well as being a person of principle.

MARY: Oh, I know that: no need to tell me. You won't be ten minutes in heaven before you're not talking to God. (*In wry despair*) I dunno what to do with you.

DRUMM (*Raising his glass*): To both of us.

MARY: Until the next time.

DRUMM: No, no: I promise. I will never again let myself be provoked.

(HE *drinks*. SHE *opens her mouth to make an angry retort, then gives him up as hopeless*)

DRUMM (*Continued*): An Irishman's claret: no finer drink.

MARY: You haven't noticed my room.

DRUMM: Haven't I? (*Looking about him*) Oh, yes.

MARY: We did it up with the compensation.

DRUMM: It has taste.

MARY: And got the few new bits of furniture.

DRUMM: I approve.
MARY: High time, says you.
DRUMM: I don't say. I felt always at home here.
MARY: It was too dark. The old people, them that's dead and gone, they went in for that: no sunlight, everything morose and dusty. I thought we'd get into the fashion.
DRUMM: You did.
MARY: We never set foot in here except for Christmas and funerals. That was the style in them days: one room for living in and another that was a museum for cracked cups. The Room, we called it. "Who's that at the door?" "Father Creedon." "Bring him into the Room."
DRUMM (*Smiling*): Yes.
MARY: I made a clearance. It's queer. The furniture was easy got rid of: out the door and that was that. But the smell of beeswax and the lavender bags my mother filled the house with: nothing'll budge that, it'll bury all of us. Still, we use the room now, by me song we do. And I had the kitchen done up as well. Do you remember how it was?
DRUMM: I know how it was.
MARY: See if you recognise it. Come on.

(THEY *start out of the room*)

MARY (*Continued*): Do you remember the old range and the dresser and the one tap over the sink?
DRUMM (*Humouring her*): Not all gone?
MARY (*Pleased with herself*): You'll see. In you go.

(*During this*, THEY *cross into the area at Left, passing the foot of the steps as if walking across a hallway. As* THEY *enter this area, lights come up. We are looking at the kitchen of forty years ago, with the dresser, the range and the cold-water earthenware sink as mentioned by* MARY. *At the kitchen table are* MIBS *and* DESMOND, *who watches as* SHE *reads silently from a book, her lips moving. There are exercise books and pen and ink.* DRUMM *looks at the young* MIBS *as* MARY *talks artlessly about the room as it is now*)

MARY (*Continued*): What do you think of it? Mr. Comerford

put in the kitchen unit and the shelves, but they had a fierce job with the new sink and the hot-and-cold, and as for the washing machine, don't talk to me. Anyhow, with that done I thought I might as well be the divil for style and break the bank altogether, so I got the new table and chairs.

DRUMM (*Only half paying attention, looking at* MIBS): You've done wonders.

MARY: At our age, what harm in a bit of comfort?

DRUMM: None.

MARY: If we don't spoil ourselves, no one else will. (*Prompting him*) So what do you think?

(DRUMM, *standing behind* MIBS, *touches her hair*)

MIBS: Stop that.

DESMOND: Sorry.

MARY: Do you like it?

DRUMM: I'm sorry. It shines. What's that odious new word, that jargon they're so fond of? Functional. It functions.

MARY (*Flatly*): I see.

DRUMM: I meant that the word was odious, not the room.

MARY (*Coldly*): Yes, I know.

DRUMM: Once it was for living in, now you cook in it and wash clothes. It suits its purpose. Formica surfaces, a refrigerator, yellow cupboards—

MARY (*Almost snapping*): They're primrose.

DRUMM: Are they? (*With false enthusiasm*) So they are.

MARY: I'm sure you're interested.

DRUMM: Mary, you must never ask a man to give you an opinion of a kitchen. Dolly now would be over the moon about it.

MARY: Dolly has taste. You left your drink.

(*Still mildly affronted,* SHE *leads the way back to the living room*)

DRUMM: It's become a new house. What it cost you, I—

MIBS (*Pushing her book aside*): I can't make head or tail of it.

(DRUMM, *on the point of leaving, looks back at her*)

DESMOND: It's simple.

MIBS: To them with brains.
DESMOND: Show me.
(DRUMM *follows* MARY *into the living room*)
MIBS: This bit. (*Reading*) "My friends, we will not go again . . ."
DESMOND: ". . . or ape an ancient rage,
Or stretch the folly of our youth to be the shame of age."
MIBS: What's it mean?
DESMOND: "Ape an ancient rage." The writer—Chesterton—what he's saying is that it's only natural for young people to be wild and passionate. (*Almost blushing*) Angry, that is. And no one minds foolishness, because it's too soon yet for them to be wise.
MIBS: But *you* are.
DESMOND: No. I'm intelligent; there's a difference. But an elderly person who behaves as if he were still young: that's . . . well, it's not nice to see.
MIBS: That's what this means?
DESMOND: Mm.
MIBS: Pity he didn't say so, then. No, it's me: I'm thick.
DESMOND: Never.
MIBS: Behind the door when the brains were handed out. Is that why you don't see old people kissing and stuff?
DESMOND: Well, what Chesterton was—
MIBS: I mean, is it because they don't like to be seen doing it, or because they're old and don't feel like doing it?
DESMOND (*Embarrassed*): Well, a mixture, I'd say.
MIBS: Imagine being kissed by someone who's all wrinkled and gubby. (SHE *thinks about it and shudders*) Eeagh!
DESMOND (*Picking up the book*): The next line—
MIBS: And anyway, kissing is one thing, but whether they want to or not, they can't . . . you know.
DESMOND: What?
MIBS: Do anything. They're not able.
(HE *conceals his discomfiture by staring into the book*)
MIBS (*Continued*): At least the man isn't. The woman doesn't have to do a hand's turn; she has it easy. (SHE *giggles*) It's a tough old station for fellows, isn't it? You

start off in life by not being able to, and you end up by not being able to. It's a panic. (*Noticing him*) You're going red.
DESMOND: No such thing.
MIBS: Y'are so, you're on fire. (*Teasing him*) Answer this and answer true: Will you love me when I'm old and grey?
DESMOND: Yes. Yes, I will.
(HE *replies so gravely and with such directness that it is her turn to be taken off-balance*)
MIBS (*Deciding to make light of it*): Is that a fact?
DESMOND: I've said so.
MIBS: Honest to God, like? No, tell us.
(HE *is silent, not knowing how to rise to her tone*)
MIBS (*Continued*): You'd want to watch out I might believe you. (*Affectionately*) Chancer. You are: you're a fierce chancer, you know that?
DESMOND (*Returning to his book*): We ought to get on with this. (HE *reads*) "My friend, we will not go again or ape an ancient rage . . ."
MIBS: Ah, quit it. My brains are in bits.
DESMOND: We're nearly done. Four more lines.
MIBS: Let me off them.
DESMOND: Two minutes.
MIBS: You will: you can't refuse me.
(SHE *makes to put the book to one side*)
DESMOND: Don't do that.
MIBS: I'll give you a kiss.
DESMOND: No.
MIBS: What?
DESMOND: I said no.
MIBS: And that's the fellow that lets on he loves me.
DESMOND: I don't buy affection, thank you.
MIBS (*Mimicking him*): "I don't buy affection, thank you." God, talk about a dry old stick. Do you know what they call you in the town? Do you know their nickname for you?
DESMOND: Because you can't have your own way—

MIBS: Mammy Cough-Bottle. It suits you.
DESMOND: "Or stretch the folly of our youth to be the shame of age . . . But walk with clearer eyes and ears this path that wandereth, And see undrugg'd in evening light the decent inn of death."
MIBS: Mammy Cough-Bottle.
DESMOND: Chesterton saw death as a country inn.
MIBS: Did he.
DESMOND: A place of shelter.
MIBS: Wasn't he great.
DESMOND: He employs a metaphor.
MIBS: What night's her night off?
(HE *slams the book down with just enough force to make her jump in spite of herself. A moment's pause*)
MIBS (*Continued*): Don't do a sulk.
DESMOND: You'll fail that exam.
MIBS: There's a blue moon out: we agree at last!
DESMOND: And you could pass it.
MIBS: No bother. Like winking.
DESMOND: You have a good mind. Fine, quick—
MIBS: And demented. You've druv me distracted. I get up in the morning and there's a looking glass in the door of the wardrobe, and I look in it and there's this person staring back at me. But it's not the person you see. God knows what *she* looks like.
DESMOND: You make difficulties.
MIBS: Yourself and bloody Chesterton: I'm unfortunate with the pair of yous.
DESMOND: He's easy.
MIBS: I'm sure. For them that had a schoolmaster for a da, yeah.
DESMOND: That has nothing to do with it.
MIBS: Not much, not half. He beat it into you. Lar Kearns told me.
DESMOND: That ignoramus.
MIBS: He says—
DESMOND (*Jealous*): When did you see him?
MIBS: He says you were never let out after tea. You were kept

in, and your da would take a cane and flay the legs off you. He says the roars of you—
DESMOND: He's a liar.
MIBS: The whole town knew it. Your da used to crease you.
DESMOND: I never roared; *that's* a lie.
MIBS: My da gave me the strap once.
DESMOND: When?
MIBS: I came home at all hours: missed the last tram and had to foot it out. I was sixteen. I walked in the door and he was weak from worrying. He asked if anyone had laid a finger on me, and when I told him no he murdered me.
DESMOND: My father . . .
(HE *hesitates*)
MIBS: What?
DESMOND: It was in case the other boys might think I was his favourite. He wanted to show them how fair he was.
MIBS: Well?
DESMOND: So he'd pretend I was daydreaming or whispering or copying answers. "Drumm, get out here."
MIBS (*Fascinated*): Leave off.
DESMOND: And always on the legs, never the hands, because he wanted to be sure I could do homework.
MIBS: My da would have gone to the school.
DESMOND: I lacked that advantage.
(MIBS *gives a small giggle*. SHE *is listening intently*)
DESMOND (*Continued*): He gave me extra subjects, you see. Three hours each evening, and he'd examine me next morning, before school. He wanted me to win scholarships. A teacher's son, he said, a boy with brains, ought to be ashamed to be paid for. If my work was poor, if it was slipshod, he'd take the cane out and lift my chin up with the tip of it. He'd say: "I want you to know why I'm doing this. Let the others, the duds, the idlers, let them work in tramyards or on the roads or draw the dole. Let them live in public houses when they have money and on street corners when they have none. But not you, by Christ, no!" . . . excuse me. "An education, that's what puts the world inside of you. And in time to come you'll

cry salt tears of gratitude for this, for I'm the only man you'll ever call your master." He used a thin cane, the sort we nicknamed a whistler. (HE *smiles*) I was the envy of the class because I was the first boy to be in long trousers. Do you know, he's dead these nine years?

MIBS: He was killed, wasn't he?

DESMOND: Mm.

MIBS: In the tunnel.

DESMOND: Yes.

MIBS: Were you sad?

DESMOND: The first thought I had was: no cane tomorrow.

MIBS (*Insisting; sentimental*): Ah. And then you were sad.

DESMOND: I think I was. I was fifteen, and I wanted the moon and couldn't have it. I wanted my father alive and myself an orphan.

MIBS (*Grinning*): Chancer.

DESMOND: Truly.

MIBS: Still, you got on, thanks to him.

DESMOND: How, got on?

MIBS: If he hadn't been so hard on you, you wouldn't be made for life today.

DESMOND (*Amused*): Is that what I am?

MIBS: My da says so. He says the civil service is a bobby's job. He says you'll be a great catch.

DESMOND (*Not displeased*): I'm sure.

MIBS: Someday.

DESMOND: He said that?

MIBS (*Airily*): For someone.

DESMOND: Nonsense.

MIBS: Whoever she is. (*Then*) Of course, the way my da drops a hint, if it fell on your head, it'd kill you.

DESMOND (*Fishing*): What hint? What about?

MIBS (*Mimicking again*): "What hint? What about?" You're so innocent you'll skip Purgatory, won't you? Anyway, I'm not going to get married, not to anyone, and least of all to you, so you needn't ask me.

DESMOND: I won't.

MIBS: You bugger. No, you're too milk-and-watery for me: there's a nun inside of you.
DESMOND: A what?
MIBS: There is.
DESMOND (*Apparently amused*): Really?
MIBS: Mm.
DESMOND: A nun.
MIBS: A Carmelite.
  (*The fixed smile on his face begins to fall apart*)
MIBS (*Continued*): Well, it's time you were told.
DESMOND: I daresay it is. (HE *makes a show of looking at his watch*) Good heavens, speaking of time—
MIBS: Now you're in a wax.
DESMOND: Not at all.
MIBS: You're raging.
DESMOND: Nothing of the sort. Only I think I ought to be—
MIBS: Take a joke.
DESMOND: I do: honestly.
MIBS: Then where are you going?
DESMOND: Home to the convent.
MIBS (*Moving to intercept him*): Ah, you messer, come back. Yes, you will, do as you're bid. Now sit.
DESMOND: I have to go.
MIBS: Don't tell lies: sit. Now listen. Why do you pick on me to persecute? We're night and day, chalk and cheese: I'm not your sort. So why?
  (HE *looks dumbly at her*)
MIBS (*Continued*): What's the fatal attraction?
DESMOND: You're a—
MIBS: Go on.
DESMOND: —very fine type of person.
MIBS (*Gently mocking*): Would you say?
DESMOND: Mind, I'm not a fool. The first time I saw you in the town I said to myself: She's human, she'll have faults like anyone else. And it's true. I mean, you fritter your time away on such rubbish. You moon over the latest crooner on the wireless and whatever the most slobbery

song is. Your head is full of film stars with their divorces and carryings-on. You have a mind like a mayfly. You don't read. That's one thing I can't understand: whenever I open a book it's the start of a journey. And you talk to cornerboys like Lar Kearns—do you know he goes into Finnegan's? Well, it's no wonder you've picked up the habit of talking about people's . . . bodies and such. Honestly!

MIBS (*Straight-faced*): But I'm a fine type of person.

DESMOND: Oh, yes.

MIBS: And the pair of us are a match, you'd say?

DESMOND: That's what I'm telling you.

(SHE *bunches up her fist and puts it to his chin as* MARY *did with* DRUMM *in the preceding scene*)

MIBS: I'll do it yet. You see if I don't.

DESMOND: Do what?

MIBS: I'll—(SHE *is seized by an uncontrollable urge to laugh.* SHE *splutters and turns away from him*) Oh, go home.

DESMOND: And that's another little fault of yours: you fly into moods for no reason.

MIBS: Will you buzz off?

DESMOND: Before I go—

MIBS: Good-bye.

DESMOND: Please. If you'll allow me, it'll make the whole evening seem worthwhile.

MIBS: Will it?

DESMOND: Let me.

MIBS: Well, don't take all night about it.

(SHE *closes her eyes and waits for the kiss. Instead, and without looking at her,* HE *sits at the table and picks up the book of verse*)

DESMOND: The last two lines; one minute, I promise you.

MIBS (*Outraged*): Oh, for God's sake.

DESMOND: "For there is good news yet to hear and fine things to be seen, Before we go to Paradise by way of—"

(*There are three loud knocks at the door opening on the backyard*)

MIBS (*Jumping*): What's that? (*A low, eerie moaning is heard*)
MIBS (*Continued*): Oh, Sacred Heart, what is it? (*The door opens slightly*)
MIBS (*Continued*): Go 'way. Desmond, save me, don't let it come in.
  (LAR KEARNS *sticks his head in*)
LAR: How are you, Mibs? I bet that shook you, what?
MIBS: It's you. (*Pleased to see him*) You bugger, you: I'm not worth me salt. (*To* DESMOND) It's Lar.
DESMOND (*Coldly*): Is it?
LAR (*Noticing him*): Ah, bejay, will you looka who's here.
  (*As* HE *crosses to greet* DESMOND, *lights dim on the kitchen and come up quickly on the living room, where* KEARNS *has entered and, in a kind of mirror image, is crossing to* DRUMM)
KEARNS: It's the Cough-Bottle himself. The dead arose and appeared, what?
MARY: That's what *I* said.
KEARNS: Me old flower, put it there.
  (DRUMM *allows his hand to be shaken.* KEARNS *is his contemporary: a feckless, good-humoured man, physically gone to seed*)
KEARNS (*Continued*): Well, it's high time you came to see us. We missed you. Are you in form?
DRUMM: I'm told so.
KEARNS (*Looking from* ONE *of them to the* OTHER): And the hatchet's buried, what? The pipe of peace is lit, yes.
DRUMM (*Querulously to* MARY): He takes me for a Mohican.
KEARNS: And the war drums is silent. Drums . . . Drumm, that's a good one. Boom-boom. (*To* MARY) Did you offer him a jar?
MARY: Certainly I offered him a—
DRUMM: I don't want another one.
KEARNS: Yes, you do. Where's his glass?
DRUMM: My dear man, will you realise that there are people in the world who, unlike yourself, mean what they say?

KEARNS: Sure I know: you meet all sorts.
(HE *busies himself pouring drinks*)
MARY (*Signalling to* DRUMM): Take it, to please him. (*To* KEARNS) And don't you go pouring for yourself.
KEARNS: Only the one.
MARY: No.
KEARNS: So's the occasion won't go by unmarked.
MARY: I 'clare to God, if the cat died he'd drink to the repose of its soul.
KEARNS: Stop growling.
MARY: He's been in Finnegan's since half-twelve. Well, it won't be the first time his dinner had to be thrun out.
KEARNS (*Handing* DRUMM *a drink*): You see what I put up with? It's the price of me for spoiling her.
MARY (*Mock anguish*): God forgive him.
KEARNS: I ought to have borrowed a page from your book. Dolly soon found out who the boss was. You used the whip from the first fence on, and now she's afraid to look crossways at you.
DRUMM: Is that meant to be funny?
KEARNS: That's where I slipped up: too much of a softy. Is it what?
DRUMM: That remark is untrue and impertinent. Dolly has never been afraid of me.
KEARNS (*Grinning*): He's a terror.
DRUMM: Certainly not with cause. She's timid by nature, highly strung, I grant you that. But to imply that I bully her—
MARY: Lar is joking.
DRUMM: Is he? I think not. And I'm sorry, but I do take exception. I despise tyrants, domestic or otherwise.
MARY: Sure we know. (*Glaring at* KEARNS) Trust you.
KEARNS: Trust me to what? Where's the harm in telling a man he wears the trousers? (*To* DRUMM) You're as prickly as bedamned: it's like talking to a gorse bush. Listen . . . good health. Delighted to see you. (HE *swallows most of his own drink with evident enjoyment*)
MARY: That's him. A glass in his hand and not a care in the

world. You're talking to us again after six years and he's not even inquisitive enough to ask why.
KEARNS: What's there to ask? He's here and he's welcome. (*To* DRUMM) You'll stay and have a bite of dinner with us.
MARY: No, he will not. Dolly has his own ready for him.
KEARNS: Good oul' Dolly. How is she? Is she tiptop?
DRUMM: She went over the summit sometime ago. (*Relenting*) She's well.
KEARNS: And how's the pen-pushing?
DRUMM: If by that you mean work, I retire in August.
MARY: You never.
KEARNS: The oul' pension at long last, what?
MARY (*Incredulous*): No, it's years away.
DRUMM: August fifth.
KEARNS: Not to mention the spondulicks into your fist.
DRUMM: It's called a gratuity.
KEARNS: Begod, but some fellows are rightly steeped, what? That's one of the disadvantages of being unemployed. There's no retirement age.
DRUMM (*Ignoring him, to* MARY): Ten more weeks.
MARY: It's true, it's true. The minutes crawl; it's the years that run.
KEARNS: Answer me this, though. (*He prods* DRUMM *with his finger and thrusts his face forward so that* THEY *are nose to nose*) Here's the question. Where does the time go?
DRUMM (*Snapping*): What?
KEARNS: The time. Tell us.
DRUMM: Much of it goes in listening to banalities.
KEARNS: Oh, yeah?
DRUMM: Uttered by buffoons.
KEARNS: You're right: too bloody true. (HE *reaches for the bottle*)
MARY: So what'll you do?
DRUMM: Do?
MARY: With your time. I suppose you have it all cut-and-dried as usual.
DRUMM: I did my sums the other day. I discovered that I

have been eight times around the world. Two hundred and ten thousand miles. Unfortunately, it was as a passenger of the Dalkey to Westland Row train. Dolly says that now is our chance to visit Stella and her husband in Toronto.
MARY: You ought to.
DRUMM: She can go. I doubt if Canada and myself would see eye to eye.
KEARNS: Did it offend you?
DRUMM: Those who have been there tell me it wants for character. I get the impression of the great outdoors and next to nothing indoors.
MARY: You'll see Stella and the children.
DRUMM: She has four now.
MARY: I heard.
DRUMM: They were with us last summer. You may have seen the boys in the town: they looked like pygmy lumberjacks. As for Stella, she's always been a rather colourless girl. Too docile; like her sister, like Una. Perhaps Canada and she were destined for each other. I've come to think of her as a kind of walking Ontario.
MARY (*Reproachful*): Desmond.
DRUMM: No, I'll stay here.
MARY: You're not natural.
DRUMM: I beg to differ. I'm fond of both my children, but that fondness doesn't blind me to the fact that through some perverse biological quirk they favour their mother. I realised it in Una's case on the day of her confirmation. I am reliably told that when she was asked if she renounced the devil and his works and pomps, she blushed and said: "I don't mind." As for Stella, I ask her how she is; she tells me, and thereafter our conversation consists of a torrent of two words every half hour. Hardly worth crossing the Atlantic for.
MARY: But you'll let Dolly go?
DRUMM: It'll be a holiday for her. And perhaps the change of air will blow some of the bees out of that bonnet of hers. She wants a motorcar.

MARY: The style of her.
DRUMM: She gets worse with age.
MARY: How?
DRUMM: A car.
MARY: Buy it for her.
DRUMM: You're as bad as she is.
MARY: Don't be so mean.
DRUMM: It's a whim. She lives two hundred yards from a bus stop. She has no need of a car.
KEARNS: Ah, but there's places a bus can't take you.
DRUMM: What? (*As previously, this is almost a bark of hostility*)
KEARNS: Halfway up Booterstown Avenue.
DRUMM: What about it?
KEARNS: You can't get there be the bus.
DRUMM: Well?
KEARNS: A motorcar's your only man.
DRUMM: What have I to do with Booterstown Avenue?
KEARNS: You can get the Stillorgan bus that passes the top of it, or you can take a Number Eight or a Seven-A to the other end. But for any place in between the two you have to hoof it.
DRUMM: Hoof it where?
KEARNS: I'm telling you. Up Booterstown Avenue.
DRUMM: Are you mad?
KEARNS: To call on people.
DRUMM: I don't know anyone on Booterstown Avenue.
KEARNS: I'm not surprised.
  (DRUMM *stares at him in fury, then turns to* MARY)
DRUMM: Of course, what's behind this is, she wants to queen it in front of the neighbours—
KEARNS: You'd walk your feet off to the knees.
DRUMM: —and thinks that I'm going to be her unpaid chauffeur.
KEARNS: We're getting a car.
DRUMM: *You* are?
KEARNS: I was thinking of a Vauxhall.
MARY (*Smiling*): Don't mind him.

KEARNS: You won't laugh when I drive up in it. (*To* DRUMM) I'm putting in for a job as a rep. Car supplied.
MARY (*Winking at* DRUMM): I'm sure you'll get it.
KEARNS: You wait.
MARY: At your age.
KEARNS: Me age is me trump card. An employer knows he can trust a man with snow on his thatch, a man that'll do a day's work and not go chasing bits of stuff. And I know the ins and outs of commodities. Didn't I travel for six months for Swinnertons' in kitchen implements?
DRUMM: You did? When?
MARY: He means the potato peelers.
KEARNS: A toppin' little gadget.
DRUMM: You hawked them, door to door.
KEARNS: I travelled, I was on the go. You're so hot with words: was I moving or wasn't I? I was my own worst enemy on that job. I could have swung the lead: instead, I saturated half the county. No one left to sell them to. Dolly bought one.
DRUMM: I know: it broke.
KEARNS: The time herself got the compensation, we coulda had a car then, only she wanted the house done up. I said to her: "You're the one that got the going-over: you spend the money."
MARY: He did: it's true.
KEARNS: "Buy whatever you like with it, even if it's a kept man."
MARY: He said that, too.
KEARNS: I mean, fair's fair. She got a fierce old knock. "Right," says I, "do the house up. I won't touch a ha'penny."
DRUMM: I'm impressed.
MARY: He's not the worst of them.
DRUMM: I'm bound to say I wouldn't have given you that much credit. I apologise.
KEARNS: Ah, dry up.
DRUMM: No, no: I lack charity.

KEARNS: I won't forget that night in a hurry. I thought she was dead.
DRUMM: You saw the accident?
KEARNS: Did I see it!
MARY: It's over and done with.
KEARNS: Begod, I saw it.
MARY: Now that'll do.
KEARNS (*Heartily*): Who do you think ran over her?
DRUMM: What?
KEARNS: You don't know?
MARY (*Uneasily*): Desmond doesn't want to—
KEARNS: Give you a laugh. Sister of mine that lives the far side of Athboy, off in the bloody wilds—her second youngest is getting married, and of course guess who's invited. "We'll go in style," says I to your one here, "or not at all." So I get the lend of Joe Duggan's car: the mini. Slip him a few quid: the job is right. Well, we have a good day of it: the Mass, the breakfast and the few harmless jars, and at the end of the story back we come: not a feather out of us. Grand. So I pull up outside Joe's house and your woman gets out to open the gate for me, so's I can reverse in, like.
MARY: I go behind the car—
KEARNS: Will you let me tell it.
MARY: It wasn't his fault.
(DRUMM *is motionless, waiting for* KEARNS *to finish*)
KEARNS: The clutch pedal is so worn me foot slips off it. Well, the car gives an almighty buck-jump backwards, and next thing she's pinned against the pillar of the gate.
MARY: Joe Duggan had no business lending that car to people.
KEARNS: Mercy of God she wasn't killed.
DRUMM: Yes, it was.
KEARNS: Still, it could happen a bishop.
DRUMM: I'm sure—if he was drunk at the time.
KEARNS: Ah, now . . .
MARY: Lar wasn't—

DRUMM: You maim the woman for life, and then you have the gall, the impudence to put on airs because you magnanimously allow her to spend her own money as she chooses.

MARY: You weren't there. You don't know what happened.

DRUMM: I know this much: that if he were ever at a wedding and came home sober, there would be a prima facie case for an annulment. (*To* KEARNS) As long as I've known you you've been a millstone around her neck: soft, easy and worthless, an idler whose idea of hard work was having to stoop to pick up his dole money. I thought that trying to cripple her spirit would be enough for you, but apparently not: you wanted to break her body as well. I'm not surprised the boy left home.

(*A pause.* KEARNS *stares at* DRUMM; *then the moment passes.* HE *laughs, shaking his head*)

KEARNS: God, Dezzie, you're a queer harp. (*To* MARY) I'll go and give me hands a rub.

MARY: Are you all right?

KEARNS: Oh, a shocker. (*He goes out*)

DRUMM: You see? No answer.

MARY: If you please, I want you to go.

DRUMM: You're upset. I'm not surprised.

MARY: You haven't changed and you never will. More fool me for thinking you could.

DRUMM: Are you saying you're vexed? With me?

MARY: I have a dinner to get.

DRUMM: Because I tell the truth?

MARY (*Angrily*): You and your truth, I'm sick of yous. Take it home with you. Pour it over your leg of lamb. Bring it to bed with you and warm your feet on it.

DRUMM: Old age hasn't made you less contrary.

(SHE *faces away from him, waiting for him to leave*)

DRUMM (*Continued*): Very well. I'll leave you for a day or so.

MARY: I don't want you back here.

DRUMM: Nonsense. (*His smile disappears as* HE *realises that she means it*) Or perhaps it isn't. (*Affronted*) As

you wish. (HE *puts his coat on, watching as* HE *does so for a sign that* SHE *may relent. Her face is tight with anger*) You know this is foolishness.
MARY: I won't have Lar talked to like that, by you or anyone.
DRUMM: I don't see the crime in saying what every inhabitant of this town over the age of reason knows to be true. He is weak, shiftless and irresponsible. It's hardly a secret.
MARY (*Wearily*): Will you go away.
DRUMM: I really don't understand you. (HE *goes to the door and stops*) Would it change matters if—
MARY: No.
DRUMM: —if I were to tell you—
MARY: I said no.
DRUMM: I don't thank you for this. You force it upon me. If I'm forbidden the house it'll be on your conscience, and I'll not have that on mine. I don't thank you at all. Ben Mulhall gives me less than six months to live. Now am I to go?
(*The lights fade slowly. As if in counterpoint, music is heard: a vocal of "You Can't Stop Me from Dreaming." The lights come up in the kitchen.* LAR *is winding up a portable gramophone, while* DESMOND *is at the table resenting his presence*)
LAR: It's real hi-de-hi stuff, wha'?
DESMOND: Pardon me?
LAR: Hi-de-hi, ho-de-ho, like.
DESMOND: I didn't know you were a linguist.
LAR: Yeah, Fred Astaire the second.
(MIBS *comes in.* SHE *has been getting ready to go for a walk*)
MIBS: Who put that thing on?
DESMOND (*Virtuously*): I didn't.
MIBS (*Turning the gramophone off*): Lar Kearns, do you not know what day it is? If me ma and da walked in they'd skin me.
LAR: Wha'?
MIBS: Can you not be like Desmond and sit quiet till I've me coat on? Messer. (SHE *goes out*)

LAR: Holy Thursdays is brutal.
DESMOND: Is they?
LAR: All the picture houses shut and no hops. Tomorrow's worse: it's Good Friday.
DESMOND: Never.
LAR: Oh, yeah: it's the day after.
(DESMOND *looks at him quizzically*)
LAR (*Continued*): After Holy Thursday, like.
DESMOND: Ah.
LAR: Peculiar day, Good Friday: give you the hump. Me and the lads, we go down to the Lady's Well and play blackjack for ha'pennies. It's sorta like stayin' out of the way till it's over. J'ever notice how if you say a curse on Good Friday it doesn't sound right?
DESMOND: Amazing.
LAR: True as God. Try it.
DESMOND: I must.
LAR: You don't go to hops?
(DESMOND *shakes his head*)
LAR (*Continued*): Y'ought to. It's how you get off your mark. I do always get up for the slow waltz: you know, when there's only the coloured lights goin' all over the place, like in the pictures when there's a jail break. Last Sunday in Dun Laoghaire town hall, "The Missouri Waltz," I got a great old lie in. Massive.
DESMOND: I'm sure it was.
LAR: A nurse. I couldn't see her home on account of she was on a bike, but I got a promise for Easter Monday. Don't tell Mibs.
DESMOND: Mary? Why not?
LAR: Spoil me chances.
(DESMOND *looks at him with hostility*)
LAR (*Continued*): No flies on Jembo. No names, no p— Wha's up?
DESMOND: In your pocket.
LAR: Where?
DESMOND: Is that a pencil?
LAR: Yeah.

DESMOND: I thought it was. Where'd you find it?
LAR: I didn't find it. It's mine.
DESMOND: Yours? (*With the air of one solving a mystery*) Ah, I see. You draw, do you?
LAR: No, it's for—(HE *realises that* HE *is being insulted. Easily*) Ah, that's good, that's quick, I like that. Sure I'm not a scholar, Dezzie: I never let on to be. (HE *takes out the pencil*) Do you know what this is for? I help me cousin Mattie that has the fishin' boat; I count the catch for him. That and tickin' off winners. Couldn't even write a Christmas card to save me life. (*Still pleasantly*) Mind, if I could, at least there's people I could send them to.
(MIBS *returns*. SHE *has her coat on*)
MIBS: Maybe I ought to wait for them. Do you think?
LAR: What time did they go out at?
MIBS: Eight.
LAR: Sure doing the Seven Churches'll take till all hours. (HE *hands her the pencil*) Here, write them a note.
(SHE *tears a page from one of the exercise books on the table*)
MIBS: Desmond says he has to be off home.
LAR (*Pleased*): Can you not come with us? Aw.
DESMOND: I don't *have* to be anywhere.
(LAR *signals to him not to stay*. DESMOND *pointedly ignores him*)
DESMOND (*Continued*): It's a good idea. A breath of fresh air. (*To* LAR, *as if not taking his point*) Yes?
MIBS (*Scribbling*): "Gone . . . for . . . a stroll."
DESMOND: Two *l*'s.
MIBS: There, short and sweet. So where'll we go?
DESMOND (*A jibe at* LAR): Good heavens, need you ask? To a "hop."
MIBS: The very thing. Where . . . the Metropole? No, the Gresham for style, seeing as I have me fur coat on.
LAR: Why don't we?
MIBS: What?
LAR: Go to a hop. You think we can't? (HE *snaps shut the*

catches on the portable gramophone and carries it towards the door) Come on . . . I'll show yous.
MIBS: Will you stop acting the—
(HE *starts out, perhaps by way of the living room, where* DRUMM *and* MARY *are, and where the lights now come up*)
MIBS: Lar, you're not to take that out of the house. It's me ma's . . . she'll reef me.
LAR (*Calling back*): Sorrento Park.
MIBS: No, bring it back. Lar!
(SHE *follows him out.* DESMOND *picks up his coat and is unaware for the moment that* SHE *has gone*)
DESMOND: I told you he was a cornerboy, but of course, you knew better. Now you can—(HE *hurries out after her. During the following, lights come up on the bandstand.* LAR *appears and sets up the gramophone on the balustrade.* HE *takes a record out of the storage space in the lid, puts it on the turntable and begins to wind up the gramophone*)
DRUMM: Nice news for a Sunday morning.
MARY: I think you're drawing the longbow.
DRUMM: Do I ever?
MARY: Ben Mulhall never said that to you.
DRUMM: He hummed and hawed, of course. I told him to waste his own time if he wished, but not mine, that I wanted none of his verbal placebos.
MARY (*Insistent*): He never said it straight out.
DRUMM: I told him, I said to him: "Look here, my friend, I was at the altar this morning, but one more word, one syllable of prevarication from you, and I shall unhesitatingly hurl myself into a state of mortal sin and you into eternity." That changed his tune for him. (HE *chuckles*)
MARY: May God forgive you.
DRUMM: Eh?
MARY: What are you laughing at?
DRUMM (*A small bemused gesture*): I suppose at what I can.
MARY: Coming here to frighten a body. I don't believe any of it.

DRUMM: You will.
MARY: I know you too well. You're a cod.
DRUMM: More, I would say, of a mackerel.
   (SHE *gives him an angry look*)
DRUMM (*Continued*): The . . . um, specialist recommends what he calls an exploratory operation.
MARY: Well, then!
DRUMM: Impudence. I've been a civil servant for long enough to recognise as such the instincts of a customs official. I am not a suitcase to be stared into and ransacked.
MARY: If it cured you—
DRUMM: What I have, as Ben Mulhall admitted when I managed to hack down the bush he was beating about, is in here (HE *touches his abdomen*) and it's terminal. More jargon from America. I keep expecting to arrive at a celestial Dublin Airport.
   (*In the bandstand,* LAR *mimes a compère speaking into a microphone*)
LAR: And now, ladies and gentlemen, the last dance before the raffle will be a Gents' Excuse-me.
DRUMM: It will go against me later, but if I could have just a drop more of . . . (HE *indicates his empty glass; it is as if he feared his composure might desert him. As* MARY *goes to fetch the whiskey bottle,* MIBS *and* DESMOND *arrive at the bandstand.* LAR *starts the gramophone. The lighting is from a streetlamp. It is an evening in early April;* MIBS *and* DESMOND *are warmly dressed;* LAR *wears a jacket and is tieless*)
LAR (*To* MIBS): Now isn't there a hop? Come on.
MIBS: Turn it off.
LAR (*To* DESMOND): Hey, it's the tune, the one I told you. Do you remember?
DESMOND: No.
LAR: Yes, you do. "The Miss—"
MIBS: It's Holy Week. Do you want us to be read off the altar?
LAR: Who's to hear? They're all at the devotions. (HE *dances on his own*) All the Holy Marys. Hey . . .

A LIFE Act One

(*This, as* DESMOND *gets to the gramophone and puts the brake on. A moan from the record as it slows down*)
LAR (*Continued*): Feck off, that's not yours.
DESMOND: Is it yours?
(*A moment of confrontation.* DESMOND *is between* LAR *and the gramophone.* LAR *is too easygoing to want to fight*)
LAR: Be a sport.
MIBS: Leave it off, or I'm going home. You loony, trying to get us a bad name.
LAR: It's all right for yous. Yous have coats, I'm freezin'.
(MIBS *sits on the steps.* DESMOND *makes haste to sit beside her.* LAR *blows on his hands and comes down to sit on the other side*)
LAR (*Continued*): Dead losses, the pair of you. Move over in the bed.
(MIBS *moves, obliging* DESMOND *to shift up also, so that* HE *is almost off the edge of the steps.* LAR *lights a cigarette. In the living room,* MARY *pours water into* DRUMM'S *whiskey.* HE *makes a sign when* HE *has had enough*)
MARY: He oughtn't to have told you.
DRUMM: Ben Mulhall?
MARY: He had no right.
DRUMM (*With some satisfaction*): In my case, I think he knew his man. But look here, not a word to Dolly.
MARY: Ah, now . . .
(HE *puts a finger to his lips*)
MARY (*Continued*): She'll have to know.
DRUMM: Not yet.
MARY: She's entitled.
DRUMM: I made up a story for her, days ago, just in case. A duodenal ulcer.
MARY: Desmond, why?
DRUMM: Peace of mind.
MARY: You're a nice man.
DRUMM: Not *her* peace of mind, for heaven's sake. My own.
MARY (*Blankly*): I see.

DRUMM: I did it well. I even invented some cut-and-thrust between Mulhall and me, with myself putting a flea in his ear, just to make it convincing. I should have been a novelist.
MARY: It's wrong for me to know and not her.
DRUMM: You forced my hand. Anyway, you're an exceptional woman; you have sense. Dolly is excitable and foolish; she'd make anyone's death a misery. Can't you see her? Beating a path between the chemist's and the church. And at home, the drugs and medicines set out in fearful symmetry like new ornaments. First, the cushions plumped; later on, the pillows. Sympathy and beef tea. She'll tell me hourly on the hour how vastly improved I look. She'll go about on tiptoe until my head splits. Her tenderness will saturate me like damp rot.
MARY: Nice talk. You don't know how well off you—
(SHE *stops, remembering*)
DRUMM: Don't I.
MARY: She's devoted to you.
DRUMM: Yes!
MARY: Thinks you're the be-all and the end-all.
DRUMM: I'm not disputing her affection, but I will not be at its mercy. Until I have to.
MARY: You don't deserve her.
DRUMM: The time I had pneumonia, she joked as if it were a head cold. Smiles and warm words, but the eyes of a child at the world's end. I don't want that again.
MARY (*Understanding this*): I know.
DRUMM: You'll appreciate now why I won't go to Canada. I daren't. You know how I've always had a passion for language. The pleasure of minting a sentence that's my own: not borrowed or shopworn. Yet now I have to stoop to the banality of saying of a place that I wouldn't be seen dead in it.
(HE *gives a fastidious shudder.* MARY *looks at him, not knowing what to say*)
DRUMM (*Continued*): In time, I suppose Dolly will send to

Toronto for Stella and to Rathfarnham for Una. They'll have me helpless at—
(HE *breaks off*) No . . . please.
MARY: What?
DRUMM: That's the look I don't want to see on Dolly's face.
MARY: Pity about you.
DRUMM: You're upset.
MARY: I can't come over it.
DRUMM: I agree. It's a damned imposition.
MARY (*Rallying*): Well, I don't care what Ben Mulhall says or what you say. If you turn your face to the wall, I won't.
DRUMM (*Smiling*): What will you do? Pray?
MARY: Jeer away: no one minds you. I have a great leg of St. Jude.
DRUMM: Ah, yes: hopeless cases.
MARY: He might surprise you.
DRUMM: Talk away to him: I can't hinder you. It's odd: I've been a government employee for forty years, and this will be the first time I've used pull.
MARY: You cod, you.
DRUMM: In the Department, when a man retires there's a presentation. The hat is passed. They give him a nest of tables or a set of Waterford. In August it'll be my turn, but I doubt if I'll put a strain on their pockets. I've indulged in unnatural practices with my subordinates, such as obliging them to do a day's work. But whatever it is, if it were only a fountain pen from Woolworth's, I mean to have it.
MARY: Sure won't you?
DRUMM: They won't be let off. I'll last that long.
(HE *looks at the ceiling*) Our friend upstairs . . .
MARY: Do you mean Lar?
DRUMM: Will he come down?
MARY: What you said to him, he took it to heart. You mightn't think so, but he did; I know him.
DRUMM (*His thoughts elsewhere*): I'm sure.
MARY: Will I tell him you didn't mean it?

DRUMM: Mary...
MARY: Ah, I will.
DRUMM (*There is an intensity in his voice which stops her*): I need to know what I amount to. Debit or credit, that much I am owed. If the account is to be closed, so be it; I demand an audit. Or show me the figures; I can add and subtract; I'll do my own books. A man has rights; if he is solvent, tell him. (HE *realises that* MARY *has not grasped his meaning. More calmly*) I have a most impressive title now: Keeper of Records. My enemies grow cunning. It takes a rare kind of peasant villainy to inflict injury and promotion with the same stroke of the pen. I have been a thorn in too many sides, and now I've been given a room to myself where I can antagonise the four walls and abuse the dust. In the strongroom there are files—so many, you could grow old counting them. Each one has a person's name and a number, and if I were God and breathed on them, they'd become lives. I seem to have access to everyone's file but my own.
(SHE *has been watching him rather than listening; sensing rather than understanding*)
DRUMM (*Continued*): Yes, you may tell him I didn't mean it: then I must go. And Dolly is not to be told.
DOROTHY: You can look as innocent as you like. I'm nobody's fool.
(MARY *goes out of the living room. In the bandstand area,* DOROTHY *has appeared.* SHE *wears a home-knitted tam-o'-shanter, with a woollen scarf and gloves to match.* SHE *is carrying two library books*)
DOROTHY (*Continued*): You can swear black is white, but I know what I heard.
MIBS (*To* LAR): There, didn't I tell you? Me da'll find out and burst me.
DOROTHY: What was it?
MIBS: It's our gramophone from home. He brung it.
DESMOND: Brought it.
MIBS: Do you know Desmond Drumm? And Lar... Laurence Kearns.

LAR: Howayah.
MIBS: This is a friend of mine: Dorothy Dignam.
DESMOND: How d'you do?
  (DOROTHY *is so flustered that* SHE *looks steadfastly away from him*)
DOROTHY (*Breathlessly, the first word a snub*): Hello, no, honest and truly, such a fright I got, music in the pitch-dark on a Holy Thursday, all I could think of was the Agony in the Garden. I thought I'd drop down dead, and then I said to myself, that's the tune that goes "'Way down in Missouri where you hear this melody," a funny old ghost that'd be.
  (SHE *gives a small, shrill laugh by way of providing a full stop.* DESMOND *looks at her stonily*)
MIBS: You won't split on us?
DOROTHY: For what?
MIBS: Because—
LAR: No fear of her. Here, squeeze in. Dezzie's doin' gooseberry.
MIBS: Mm, sit with us.
DOROTHY: I said I'd be home after the library . . .
LAR: Where's your rush? Dezzie, good lad, be a gent.
DOROTHY (*Looking at* DESMOND): If I'm disturbing anyone . . .
  (MIBS *nudges* DESMOND, *who gets to his feet reluctantly to give her his place*)
MIBS: You aren't. For a minute . . .
  (SHE *pats the space beside her*)
DOROTHY (*To* DESMOND, *shortly*): Thanks.
LAR: That's the dart: nothin' like an even number.
DOROTHY: I won't stay.
MIBS (*To* DESMOND): Dolly goes to the Tech in Dun Laoghaire.
DESMOND: Who does? Oh?
MIBS: She's blue-mouldy with brains . . . aren't you? She was the head of our class in the Loreto.
DOROTHY: Don't tell stories.
MIBS: You were.

DOROTHY: I was second.
MIBS: Well!
LAR: Begod, there's no doubt. Someone is well matched, wha'?
DESMOND (*Venomously*): And someone else isn't.
LAR: Steeped, so y'are.
MIBS: Desmond lives with his aunt on Nerano Road. I'm sure you know him to see.
DOROTHY (*Lying*): I don't think so.
MIBS: He's around the corner. Yes, you do.
DESMOND (*Suddenly amiable*): Why should she? I'm sure Dorothy doesn't walk about staring at people. You go to Dun Laoghaire Tech, do you?
DOROTHY: Yes.
DESMOND: Woodwork?
(SHE *makes to rise.* MIBS *holds her by the arm*)
MIBS: Don't be so smart. Dolly does . . . what?
DOROTHY: It's called Commerce.
LAR: Hey, tell yous a joke. There's this fella and this mott, and they go out to Baldonnell . . . you know, to the—
MIBS (*Indicating* DOROTHY): Now be careful.
LAR: No, it's clean: honest. They go out to the aerodrome, like. And they see this aeroplane landin'—
DOROTHY (*To* DESMOND): For your information, it's typing, shorthand, bookkeeping and senior English.
LAR: Ah, Jasus, listen.
MIBS: Don't take the sacred name.
LAR: Sorry. They take this feckin' aeroplane—
MIBS: Lar!
LAR: They see this . . . oul' aeroplane comin' down. And your woman, the mott, she says to your man: "Is that a mail plane?" And he says: "No, them's the landin' wheels."
(*There is silence for a moment. Then* MIBS *gives a snort and punches* LAR. SHE *averts her head so that* DOROTHY *cannot see her laugh*)
DESMOND: Oh, for God's sake.
LAR: Good, wha'?

A LIFE Act One 40

DESMOND: Yes, for a street corner I suppose it's—
DOROTHY: Excuse me, do you mind? (*To* LAR) And then what?
LAR: Hoh?
DOROTHY: After the landing wheels.
LAR: No, you don't get it. Your man, the fella . . . he thought that *she* thought the wheels was—
  (*In panic and to create a diversion,* DESMOND *snatches the library books from* DOROTHY)
DESMOND: These look interesting. What are they?
DOROTHY: Well, honestly.
LARS: —that she thought they were—
  (MIBS *puts a hand over his mouth*)
DOROTHY: Such manners.
DESMOND: This one's a waste of time: trash; but this isn't bad. You'll enjoy it.
DOROTHY (*Coldly*): You don't say.
DESMOND: It's not one of his best, mind. Have you read *Good-bye to All That?*
MIBS (*Suddenly*): Dolly Drumm.
DESMOND: What?
MIBS: I just remembered. It's a sort of game Dolly used to play.
DOROTHY: Mary, you're not to.
MIBS: When we were at school, like. Honestly. Whenever she'd meet a fellow, anyone, she'd put her name along with his.
DOROTHY: No, you're mean.
MIBS: To see how it would sound.
DOROTHY: It was for a joke.
MIBS: Trying it out, like.
DOROTHY: I was not.
MIBS: Dolly Drumm. God, that's the worst yet. Brutal.
  (DOROTHY *looks at the ground in embarrassment.* DESMOND *is aloof, unamused.* LAR, *restless, goes into the bandstand*)
MIBS (*Continued*): (*Laughing, to* DESMOND) That's your hash cooked for you.

Lar (David Ferry) gathers Mibs (Lauren Thompson) in his arms as, rebelling against solemnity, they dance on Good Friday.

Kearns (Pat Hingle) glows as Mary (Aideen O'Kelly) affirms his generosity in letting her spend all the compensation money —from a car accident in which he, drunk, ran her down.

Dolly (Helen Stenborg) admits that during the past six years that Drumm has been on the outs with Lar and Mary, she's paid them secret friendly visits.

Drumm (Roy Dotrice) denies his one remaining dream—to write a book about his village: "There are as many books in the world as there are fools."

Photos by Ed Ellis

DOROTHY (*Without looking up; a whisper*): Stop it.
LAR: Hey . . .
   (*As* THEY *look around,* HE *begins to sing, conducting as* HE *does so*)
LAR (*Continued*): "Good-bye, Dolly, I must leave you, Good-bye, Dolly, I must go . . ."
   (MIBS *at once joins in, motioning to him to keep his voice down.* DRUMM, *in the living room, looks around, as if suspecting mockery. After a few lines,* DOROTHY, *too, joins in, happy that the joke is over. Towards the end,* DRUMM *begins to beat out the time with his finger and hums the tune audibly. Then* MIBS *overrides the* OTHERS)
MIBS (*Loudly*): ". . . Good-bye, Dolly . . . Drumm!" (SHE *laughs and hugs* DOROTHY, *whose feelings are again hurt.* DRUMM *and* DESMOND *are* BOTH *looking at her resentfully. Her laughter as it tails off overlaps the entrance of* KEARNS *and* MARY)
MIBS (*Continued*): I'm a horror.
MARY (*Indicating* DRUMM): There he is now.
KEARNS: Dezzie, are you off? Sure put it there.
DRUMM: I was rude to you. It was uncalled for.
KEARNS: What rude? When?
DRUMM: Mind, I hold to the substance of what I said, but this is your house and I was unmannerly.
KEARNS: Will you go 'long outa that. You weren't.
DRUMM: I insulted you.
KEARNS: Not at all.
DRUMM: Are you stupid? I say I did.
MARY: Now, Desmond.
DRUMM: And I ought not to have mentioned the lad.
KEARNS: Who?
DRUMM: The boy. Young Sean.
KEARNS (*Flatly*): Sure you didn't.
   (DRUMM *turns away in exasperation*)
MARY: Now that will do. After tea, Desmond and Dolly will be coming over for an hour or so. (*To* DESMOND) Yes, you will.
KEARNS: And why the hell wouldn't they?

DRUMM: I'd like that. Thank you.
KEARNS: All together again like Brown's cows, wha'? Sure, Dezzie, do you know what I'm goin' to tell you? In this town . . . look at all the great characters we had. And you never seen such a clearance. They're all gone, except for the pair of us. You and me: that's as true as I'm standin'. Gone with the poor oul' trams. Sonny Doyle and Darley the landlord, and your own da in his time, God be good to him—
MARY: Will you let the man go to his dinner?
KEARNS: —an', an' Fanny Cash, an' Slippers we thought was the German spy. (HE *clamps an affectionate hand on* DRUMM'*s shoulder, his face at too-close range*) Meself an' yourself, the last of the good stuff. Sure they'll never bate the Irish out of Ireland.
DRUMM (*Freeing himself*): Who else would have us? (HE *puts on his raincoat. To* MARY) About Dolly. I'll give her this much: she's loyal. Our long silence, yours and mine: she had no part in it. So if she stopped coming here—
KEARNS (*Amused*): If she what?
MARY (*A warning*): Hold your tongue.
DRUMM: —that was my doing, not hers. You mustn't be cross with her.
MARY: With Dolly? Ah, get sense. (SHE *sees him to the door*)
DRUMM: Do you remember once, when you thought of taking a secretarial course?
MARY: When *you* thought.
DRUMM: I tried to teach you a poem.
MARY: And I'm sure I learnt it!
DRUMM: "My friends, we will not go again or ape an ancient rage, Or stretch the folly of our youth to be the shame of age."
MARY: What about it?
DRUMM: "But walk with clearer eyes and ears the path that wandereth, And see undrugg'd in evening light the decent inn of death." (*Gently*) It isn't a decent inn, Mary.

When you get up close, it's a kip. (HE *goes out. If possible,* HE *should remain in sight; at any rate, there should be no impression given of an "exit." In the bandstand,* LAR *is going through the other records in the lid of the gramophone. Stealthily* HE *puts one on.* DESMOND *is standing, perhaps still looking at one of the books.* MIBS *and* DOROTHY *are still seated together.* DRUMM *is seen walking to the rear of the bandstand*)

KEARNS (*Picking up his Sunday paper*): Sure poor oul' Dezzie.

DOROTHY (*To* DESMOND): I did see you in the town.

DESMOND: Pardon me.

KEARNS: I always had a great leg of him.

DOROTHY: Mary knows I did. And I knew your name and where you lived and that you were in the civil service.

DESMOND (*Indifferent*): Really.

DOROTHY: I don't know why I pretended I didn't, because I was brought up to be straight with people. So I apologise for telling lies, and if I can please have my books back I'll go home.

MIBS: Stay.

DOROTHY: No, Mary. I think I've been disappointed enough in people for one night. If you don't mind . . . (SHE *holds out her hands, waiting for* DESMOND *to return the books.* HE *is about to do so when there is a blare of music from the gramophone. It is a dance tune of the late 1930s: "You Can't Stop Me from Dreaming" or something similar*)

MIBS: Lar Kearns, you wretch. You turn that off.

LAR: You do it.

MIBS: Watch me.

(SHE *goes into the bandstand.* LAR *is between her and the gramophone.* HE *grabs her, forcing her to dance*)

MIBS (*Continued*): You messer, will you . . . will you let me go. Lar, you'll get me into trouble.

LAR: I know, but we'll have a dance first.

DESMOND: Kearns, you stop that.

A LIFE Act One

(MIBS, *yielding, begins to dance with* LAR. *Encouraged,* HE *holds her close.* DESMOND *looks on, consumed with jealousy*)

LAR: That's the girl.

MIBS: I'm going to be murdered.

LAR: Hey, Cough-Bottle, how about this for a lie-in, wha'?

DESMOND: Kearns! (HE *goes into the bandstand and makes for the gramophone*)

MIBS (*Laughing*): God, if someone sees us . . .

(DESMOND *stops the gramophone.* DRUMM *is now visible at the far side of the bandstand*)

LAR: Ah, will you put it back on.

DESMOND: You were told to stop.

LAR: Quit actin' the maggot. Fair do's now: give Dolly a dance, come on. (HE *takes a step forward*)

DESMOND: I warned you. (HE *takes the record from the turntable*)

LAR: Sure, you did.

DESMOND: I mean it.

LAR: Look, don't be such a—

(DESMOND *deliberately smashes the record.* MIBS *screams. For a moment,* DESMOND *is appalled by his own action, then, as* LAR *moves forward,* HE *attempts to take the other records from the lid.* LAR *grabs him and throws him easily to one side*)

DESMOND: You guttersnipe. (HE *rushes at* LAR, *who holds him off effortlessly.* DESMOND *strikes out at him, but every intended blow falls short*)

LAR: Easy, now. What the hell is the—

DESMOND (*Flailing*): Damn cornerboy . . . you leave her alone . . . you lout, you blackguard, I'll kill you.

(LAR *grins at the ease with which* HE *keeps him at bay.* DESMOND *is close to tears*)

DOROTHY: Mary, stop them.

MIBS: Yes. Desmond . . . Lar, will yous stop it.

(DRUMM *enters the bandstand from the rear. He shoulders his way between* DESMOND *and* LAR, *causing them to*

fall apart. HE *looks at them, his eyes filled with his own pain and anger*)
DRUMM: Be damned to the lot of you. (HE *walks down the front steps of the bandstand and goes off.* THEY *stare after him*)

CURTAIN
END OF ACT I

ACT TWO

DESMOND *is in the bandstand, alone.* HE *consults his notes, then puts them away as* DRUMM *did at the start of Act I. As an orator,* HE *lacks assurance; this is merely a rehearsal, but his voice quavers from nerves.*

DESMOND: To conclude. As from December next this country shall at . . . or is it "will"? . . . *will* at last cease to be merely a Free State and instead take its place as a free land. In place of—(*To himself*) You're rushing it: wait for applause. In place of a Governor-General, we will have a . . . no, blast it: we shall, *shall* have a President. My respectable . . . (*Almost moaning*) respec*ted* opponents have said . . . (*Under his breath*) God, make them say it! . . . that now is our opportunity to cut ourselves finally free of all that is English.
(DOROTHY *enters the bandstand behind him and listens, unnoticed*)
DESMOND (*Continued*): Mr. Chairman, I cannot understand people who hold grudges, who sulk, who cling to old wrongs and injuries. If it is in their nature, it is not in mine. I say that we should retain all that is best of the old to take with us into the new Golden Age, into the— and those of you who have been to the Picture House in Dun Laoghaire this week will grasp my meaning—into that beckoning Shangri-la of which Mr. De Valera is the two-hundred-year-old High Lama (HE *laughs, pleased at his own wit*)
DOROTHY: They'll boo you for that bit.
DESMOND (*Embarrassed*): Good evening. I was—
DOROTHY: . . . Practising. I heard.
DESMOND: There's to be a—
DOROTHY: . . . Debate, at the Harold Boys' School. I know.

DESMOND (*Annoyed*): Excuse me, but do you happen to live here?
DOROTHY: Pardon me?
DESMOND: I mean *here*. In the bushes somewhere or under a flat rock. (*As* SHE *stares at him*) I wondered.
DOROTHY: Honestly and truly, for a young man your age you're the most dreadful crosspatch.
DESMOND (*Dismissive*): Amn't I.
DOROTHY: And for your information, the reason I'm here—and excuse me for mentioning that people talking to themselves is the first sign of madness—what brought me is to say that Mary can't go with you.
DESMOND: Do you mean to the debate?
DOROTHY: She said not to wait for her and all the best.
DESMOND: Why? It was—(HE *breaks off as* DRUMM *and* DOLLY *appear.* THEY *cross towards the living room area.* DRUMM *notices* DESMOND *and* DOROTHY, *who wait until* HE *and* DOLLY *have passed*)
DOLLY (*Lagging behind, breathless*): She spent a fortune on having the house done up, paid out every penny she got from the accident. Did she show you her kitchen? The cupboards and the new washing machine and the—
(DRUMM *stops suddenly so that* SHE *all but collides with him*)
DRUMM: How do you know?
DOLLY: What? (*A small, nervous laugh*) I heard in the town.
(DRUMM *continues off, letting her pass him*)
DESMOND: Why can't she?
DOROTHY: What?
DESMOND: Come with me.
DOROTHY (*The same nervous mannerism as* DOLLY'*s*): A toothache.
DESMOND: Since when?
DOROTHY (*Embellishing*): I think it must be an abscess. She tried oil of cloves, and now her father is taking her to Mr. Corbet.
DESMOND: Who?
DOROTHY: To have it pulled.

A LIFE Act Two

DESMOND (*Dismayed*): But I wanted her to . . . (HE *leaves the sentence unfinished.* HE *will not show himself as vulnerable in front of her*)
DOROTHY: He pulled one of mine once. See? (SHE *draws back the corner of her mouth to show him*)
DESMOND: Damn.
DOROTHY (*Pointing*): Arrh?
DESMOND: Yes.
DOROTHY: Her father is dragging her there. I know she'd miles rather go and listen to you and suffer.
(HE *looks at her as if suspecting a gibe. Her face is ingenuous*)
DOROTHY (*Continued*): Really, she's as cross as two sticks. I mean, who wouldn't be? She said to me: "He'll be there, standing his ground against T.D.'s and professors out of colleges and such. The whole town will see him except me."
DESMOND: She won't miss much.
DOROTHY: Do you hear him! Anyway, she said all the best.
DESMOND: It's my first time, you know.
DOROTHY: Go on. After this, you won't talk to us.
DESMOND: Far too grand, yes.
DOROTHY: You might be. Wait till you see tomorrow's papers: you'll be a stone's throw from famous. Do you know what my father says? "Young Desmond Drumm? . . . Oh, he's a born genius."
DESMOND: Yes, I'm much liked by fathers.
DOROTHY: From this out, there'll be no stopping you. And Mary is going to be very sorry, you'll see. (*As* HE *looks at her*) I mean, even sorrier.
DESMOND: Was that a story?
DOROTHY: What?
DESMOND: About a toothache.
DOROTHY: No!
DESMOND: Because—
DOROTHY: Excuse me, I'm not in the custom of telling—
DESMOND: Because if she'd prefer to go some place less boring . . . I mean, she's free to, she needn't lie about it.

I'm not her keeper: God forbid. (*Unable to keep the question back*) I suppose she went out with him.
DOROTHY: Who?
DESMOND: Who!
DOROTHY: Do you mean Lar Kearns? You're wrong.
DESMOND: I'm sure.
DOROTHY: Well, you are wrong. Because he's going to the debate.
DESMOND (*Appalled*): He's what?
DOROTHY: With a crowd from the town. To cheer you.
DESMOND: Oh, my God.
DOROTHY: Isn't it nice of him? So there.
DESMOND: What time is it? (HE *pulls out his notes, sits on the balustrade and pores over them in an agony of stage-fright*)
DOROTHY: I thought I might go as well.
  (HE *is memorising, eyes closed, lips moving*)
DOROTHY (*Continued*): If nobody minded.
KEARNS (*To* DOLLY): Sure you're welcome.
  (DRUMM *and* DOLLY *have appeared in the living room, ushered in by* MARY. *It is very much a Sunday evening occasion: sandwiches and a cake are on the sideboard. In the bandstand,* DOROTHY *lingers, watching* DESMOND)
DOLLY: Hello, Lar. How are you?
KEARNS: Gettin' younger, the same as yourself. But sure you've been giving us the go-by for so long I wouldn't know a bit of you. Donkey's years, wha'? (HE *gives her an overdone wink of complicity*)
DOLLY (*Nervously*): Oh, now.
MARY (*A warning*): Will you take Desmond's coat off him and not leave the man standing.
KEARNS: Who's this? Another stranger, begod. Haven't clapped eyes on him since dunno when.
DRUMM: Good evening.
KEARNS: Ha-ha, quick as a flash. Give us that. (HE *takes* DRUMM'S *coat. From* MARY *and* DOLLY *there is a fusillade of small talk.* DRUMM, *who loathes whatever* HE *considers banal, looks on in disgusted fascination*)

MARY: Isn't the weather glorious?
DOLLY: Beautiful.
MARY: I'm sure the crowds of the world are out.
DOLLY: The town is black.
MARY: Such a day. I did half me wash.
DOLLY: Go 'way.
MARY: And hung it up. Dry in no time.
DOLLY: Aren't you great.
MARY: "It's a Sunday," I said. "It's a sin. I don't care."
DOLLY: These days, no one minds.
MARY: But if it was twenty years ago . . .
DOLLY: Oh, then! Oh, yes!
MARY: One stocking on a line on a Sunday . . .
DOLLY: Don't I know.
MARY: And Father Creedon 'ud be at that door.
DOLLY: Giving out to you.
MARY: He was a terror.
DOLLY (*Fondly*): Ah, Father Creedon.
DRUMM (*Who can stand no more*): Oh, good God.
DOLLY: No, it's great drying weather. (*To* DRUMM) What, pet?
DRUMM: Will you have done with this damned table tennis and look at your surroundings?
DOLLY: Where? (SHE *looks about her vaguely. It has slipped her mind that* SHE *is supposed not to have seen the room lately*)
MARY (*Prompting*): At me new room.
DOLLY: What? (*Then*) Oh. Oh, it's beautiful. Look at it, Dezzie, it's exquisite.
DRUMM: Really.
DOLLY (*Babbling*): I wouldn't know it. That's new and that's new and the wallpaper is—
MARY: Before we sit, come and look at my kitchen. Lar, give Desmond whatever he's having. Be useful. (SHE *urges* DOLLY *out of the room. As* THEY *cross towards the kitchen,* MARY *begins to laugh helplessly*)
DRUMM: That woman becomes more of a fool each day.
    (DOLLY, *although* SHE *has been shaken by her narrow es-*

cape, catches MARY's mood and laughs, too. DRUMM turns his head suspiciously. As MARY switches on the kitchen light, we see that MIBS is at the table, weeping. SHE dabs at her eyes with a handkerchief. MARY sits near her and wipes her own eyes)

DOLLY: It's not comical, it isn't.

MARY: You aren't safe to be let out on your own.

DOLLY: When he came home and said you'd invited us, I thought: I must remember now to act surprised at the house and go "ooh" and "ah" and all the rest of it. And it went clear out of my head.

MARY (*Laughing again*): "That's new," says you, "and that's new and that's new . . ."

DOLLY: Stop it, I got a fright.

MARY: If he could see you having your Friday cup of coffee.

DOLLY (*Frightened*): Will you hush.

 (KEARNS *has produced an unopened half bottle of whiskey and a six-pack of stout*)

KEARNS: I have me orders from the Commandant: no hard stuff. So you get dug into this. (HE *opens the whiskey*)

DRUMM (*Testily*): A cup of tea would have sufficed.

KEARNS: You'll get that as well. No one goes out of here sayin' they weren't asked if they had a mouth on them.

DRUMM: You're an ostentatious man.

KEARNS (*Proudly*): I am, begod.

DRUMM (*Half to himself*): And a hopeless one.

KEARNS: No, I prefer the drop of stout. The occasional ball of malt is harmless, but at my age, when there's a bit of mileage on the oul' clock, a man ought to go easy.

DRUMM: What about at *my* age?

KEARNS: You're different, Dezzie. You have acid in you. 'S a fact; it's in the canals, I studied it. You could drink Jameson's distillery dry, and you might get half-shot; but the element in the whiskey that does damage to the human liver would be nullified by the acid your system is glutted with.

DRUMM: Balderdash.

KEARNS: Laugh, I don't mind. You wouldn't be the first one to make a mock of science. The body doesn't manufacture acid for a hobby, you know.
DRUMM (*Calling*): Dolly . . .
(DOLLY, *who does not hear, is in the kitchen, talking with* MARY)
KEARNS: Still, a man's a right to mind himself. Did you hear that poor oul' Nick Tynan was brought to the chapel yesterday?
DRUMM: Who?
KEARNS: Out of Begnet's Villas. You knew him.
DRUMM: Yes. His boy, his foster son, was with me for a time; in my section, that is.
KEARNS: A great oul' warrior.
DRUMM (*Aggressive*): A what?
KEARNS: A character. There'll be a big turnout at that funeral.
DRUMM: I'm sure.
KEARNS: The chapel was packed.
DRUMM: I'd expect no less. He worked hard and lived decently, and by now he'll have given his mind back to the Almighty in the same unused condition as he received it. Why shouldn't they pack the church? All his life he ran with the herd and honoured the eleventh commandment: Thou shalt not make the rest of us seem inferior. Yes, I knew him. A man of no malice and less merit. Lord have mercy.
KEARNS: All the same, Dezzie, he was a—
DRUMM: A character, yes. It's a word used to describe any ignoramus or bigot over sixty. You'll have a most impressive funeral yourself one of these days.
KEARNS (*Pleased*): Who, me?
DRUMM: Given the existing criteria for large attendances, I've no doubt of it. Mass cards and floral tributes. Your coffin will be invisible under the wreaths of intertwined platitudes.
KEARNS (HE *looks at* DRUMM *for a moment; then, almost blushing*): How much do you want to borra?
DRUMM: Mine, I think, will be a more modest affair. The chief

mourners are likely to be a small group of unsplit infinitives.
KEARNS: Not at all. Aren't you one of our own?
DRUMM: Am I? (HE *drops the subject, almost with contempt*) Tynan's son, the boy he adopted: I took a special interest in him.
KEARNS: A brainy lad.
DRUMM: Dangerously fond of saying "yes." He needed starch in his backbone. I watched over him, took no nonsense, told him that as long as he worked for me he would pull his socks up! In the end, of course, he was a disappointment.
(KEARNS *makes to top up his drink*)
DRUMM (*Continued*): (*Covering his glass*) Leave it. I wondered afterwards why I'd bothered with him. I'm not a masochist. I don't ask to have kindnesses flung back at me, or for that matter to become an office joke. "I hear that Drumm has been let down again." How stupidly we deceive ourselves. It was because of Sean.
(KEARN'*s watery eyes become uneasy.* HE *makes a lumbering attempt to avoid the subject*)
KEARNS: I hear young Tynan is over for the—
DRUMM: He left here just about then. I suppose I missed him and made a friend of the other boy.
KEARNS: —for his da's funeral.
DRUMM: Do you hear from him? From Sean.
KEARNS: Herself does.
DRUMM: Don't you?
KEARNS: Sure he knows I read the letters. Christmas and Easter . . . he never starves us for news.
DRUMM: Is he well?
KEARNS: Tiptop, he says himself. He's teachin', you know, in a school in . . . uh, it's near London. Can't get me tongue around the name. Slow, is that it?
DRUMM: Do you mean Slough?
KEARNS: Slough! You done that for him . . . got him interested in books an' stuff. (*Grinning*) A bloody schoolteacher . . . the same as your da was.
DRUMM: Bravo.

KEARNS: Was he married when you were here last?
DRUMM: Newly married, yes.
KEARNS: Him and her, there was what you might call a separation. I dunno the ins and outs of it. Sure over there is not like here. It's all choppin' and changin': everything on again, off again, like a vest in the autumn.
DRUMM: He had no right to go, not as he did.
KEARNS: Ah, well.
DRUMM: Ah, well what?
KEARNS: That's the way o' the world.
DRUMM: Will you stop mouthing banalities? He had a life here; his people. I'd have thought better of him: it showed a want of feeling.
KEARNS: Sean and me never hit it off. Chalk an' cheese.
DRUMM (*Reluctant to seem to care*): Does he ask for me?
KEARNS: Hoh?
DRUMM: In his letters.
KEARNS: Oh, I'm sure he does.
DRUMM: Well, does he or doesn't he?
KEARNS: Yes. Oh, catch him forgettin'. "How's . . . uh, Uncle Dezzie?"

(DRUMM *glares at him, not convinced*)

KEARNS (*Continued*): There was a time I thought of makin' the trip, droppin' in to see him. But sure my travellin' days is over.
DRUMM: Your what? My dear man, I've been further around a chamber pot in search of the handle than you've travelled in your entire life. (DRUMM *hears* DOLLY *and* MARY *moving back from the kitchen*)
DOLLY: . . . He was great. He told them all about the Cat's Ladder and where Shaw lived and Sorrento Park and I don't know what else.
MARY: This morning, you say? How well he kept it to himself.

(*As* THEY *leave the kitchen,* MARY *shuts the door behind them.* MIBS *runs to it and speaks through it*)

MIBS: Daddy? Can I come out? Can I please come out and

talk to you and Mammy? (*Getting no answer,* SHE *returns and sits at the table.* DOLLY *and* MARY *enter the living room*)
MARY: I hear you've been speechifyin'.
KEARNS: Who?
MARY: Walking the legs off half the town and telling them what happened in old God's time.
DRUMM: There were two dozen people, and it wasn't a speech: it was a . . . talk.
DOLLY: Don't mind him: he was great.
DRUMM: You weren't there.
DOLLY: I saw you.
DRUMM: Now she reads lips.
DOLLY: Everyone's talking about it.
DRUMM: Who is? Name one.
MARY: That'll do. Behave yourself.
KEARNS: I remember Dezzie one time makin' a toppin' speech. Below in the Harold Boys', and that wasn't today nor yesterday.
DOLLY: Don't I know? I was there.
KEARNS: You were in me boot. You were at home in your pram.
(*A shrill laugh from* DOLLY. *In the bandstand,* DESMOND *rises, ready to face his ordeal.* MARY, *who has brought a teapot with her from the kitchen, sets about distributing the cake plates*)
MARY: And I was in me go-car. Shift your feet. Dolly, will you sit?
DOLLY: Do you hear him, Dezzie? In my pram!
KEARNS: It was so packed, we were sittin' on the windowsills. I don't forget that night.
DOROTHY: Is it the time?
(DESMOND *nods. Panic has set in*)
DOROTHY (*Continued*): Well, all the very best.
DESMOND (*Dry-mouthed*): Thank you.
DOROTHY: You've no call to be nervous. Just don't think what a great night it is for you. Pretend it isn't.

DESMOND: Mm.
DOROTHY: And I know it's none of my business, but honestly and truly I'd leave out that bit about Mr. De Valera, because it's only trying to be smart.
(DESMOND, *too nervous to heed her, begins to move Off*)
DOROTHY (*Continued*): Do you want me to walk with you? If you'd sooner go by yourself, it's a free country. One thing I was taught and I've always kept to is, never go where you're not—(SHE *realises that* HE *is moving out of earshot.* SHE *follows him Off: a walk that longs to be a run. Through this,* MARY *has been pouring tea and now offers milk and sugar*)
KEARNS: Boys, oh boys, you gev them a great talk that night.
DRUMM: Did I?
KEARNS: You damn well did. I can still hear them clappin' and cheerin' you.
DRUMM: You hear more than I did.
MARY: Excuse me. Two spoons for you, Dolly?
DOLLY: Thanks.
MARY: How? (*A small embarrassed laugh*) Like an elephant. And for yourself it's . . .
DRUMM (HE *waits a moment, calling the bluff; then*): None.
MARY (*Affecting to remember*): None.
KEARNS: Acid!
DOLLY: Dezzie says he might write a book now. About the town.
KEARNS: A book?
MARY: You'd never.
DRUMM: Dolly takes the . . . whim for the deed. I said that *someone* should—
KEARNS: No better man. Y'ought to put me in it.
DOLLY: No, it's about the olden times. History. Dezzie knows every stick and stone in the town, don't you, pet? And he has all the bits out of the papers and the old maps, albums of them in the loft, and the reams of stuff his father left.
DRUMM (*To* MARY *and* KEARNS): Fuel for a bonfire.
DOLLY (*Smiling*): Oh, I'm sure.

DRUMM: There are as many books in the world as there are fools. I don't intend to augment the ranks of either.
DOLLY: But you must do it.
DRUMM: Must?
DOLLY: You said you would.
DRUMM: It was a daydream.
DOLLY: Well, I don't see why you won't. You have all the time you want now.
(*A pause.* MARY *fetches the sandwiches and the cake.* DOLLY *looks at* DRUMM, *waiting for his response*)
DOLLY (*Continued*): The first proper history, you said. You were over the moon: yes, you were. It was all you ever talked of. (*Bitterly*) It's only because you know how pleased I'd be. A book with your name on it. If I said it was foolish or a waste of time, then you'd write it to spite me.
MARY (*Offering the food*): Dolly . . .
DOLLY: Wouldn't you? (*To* MARY, *attempting to act the role of the guest*) Oh, now, such trouble, aren't you awful?
MARY: What trouble? A bit of sweet cake. Desmond . . .
(DRUMM *takes a sandwich*)
KEARNS: Eat away. When we haven't it, we'll do without. Do you know, Dezzie, the mornin' after that evenin' the talk in the town was that you might end up runnin' the country.
DRUMM: Running from it, I think.
KEARNS: No. 'Clare to God: the whole shebang. Dolly, was he great or was he not?
DOLLY (*Still hurt*): I dunno.
DRUMM: I do.
KEARNS: You were massive. I remember.
DRUMM: Through a Guinness glass darkly.
KEARNS: Wha'?
DRUMM: Delude yourself by all means: not me. Oh yes, you were there, perched on a windowsill, and by the door I saw the gentlemen of leisure who haunted the betting shop and Gilbey's corner. And when my turn came to speak, there was what disguised itself as a cheer. I imag-

ine it was the kind of noise the Romans made when the first Christian entered the arena. I heard you shouting: "Good old . . . Mammy Cough-Bottle."

KEARNS: For a joke.

DRUMM (*Sincerely*): I know it was. I cleared my throat, and at once half the room turned consumptive. I began to speak. Someone yelled: "Can't hear you." That was the signal for a barrage of meaningless, inane catchphrases, the sort that are thrown as boys throw stones at a broken wall, to see which one brings it down. Did my mother know I was out? Who swallowed the dictionary? Did I wash my neck lately? Would I work for a farmer? Those who lacked the talent to coin epigrams merely whistled.

KEARNS: Not at all: you're dreamin'.

DRUMM: It was like a dream at the time: a bad one. My nerve went. I gabbled. I heard my voice become shrill, like a girl's. Whenever I used a word with more than two syllables, they hooted. I skipped to the end, I fled to it . . . to a facetious—I suppose a juvenile quip about De Valera. They applauded that.

KEARNS: Amn't I sayin'?

DRUMM: Yes, they clapped—slowly. May I? (HE *offers his cup for more tea*) Our chairman was the then parish priest. When he obtained order, he said: "And now that we've all had our bit of fun . . ."

KEARNS (*Laughing, meaning* DRUMM): A fierce man for drawin' the longbow.

MARY: Desmond, will you get sense? Anyplace you go, you'll find a pack o' jeers. More fool you to mind them.

DRUMM: Once it was over and I'd sat down, I didn't mind them in the least. I even saw the humour of it.

(DESMOND *runs on, in flight from the humiliation of his speech.* HE *stops by the bandstand.* HE *is shaking. In a wave of nausea* HE *grasps one of the iron pillars and begins to retch*)

DRUMM (*Continued*): I was calm, quite unperturbed. You see, I understood. It was a punishment. I had broken the eleventh commandment. I had tried to be different, to be

the clever boy, the . . . (*A look at* DOLLY) born genius. Well, they were not impressed.
DOLLY (*Suddenly*): I cried.
DRUMM: What?
DOLLY: That evening.
DOROTHY (*Calling, Off*): Desmond . . .
DRUMM: Did you? I was amused. I had discovered that cleverness was like having a deformed hand. It was tolerated as long as you kept a glove on it.
DOROTHY (*Off*): Desmond, is that you?
(DESMOND *runs off quickly towards the kitchen area.* DOROTHY *appears and follows him*)
DRUMM: I actually believed that if I spoke well and carried the argument they would admire me. I craved it. I wanted to be . . . (HE *looks at* KEARNS) one of our own. Dear God, what a contemptible ambition: to please the implacable. Well, I never gave them a second chance: I had that satisfaction. (HE *smiles at* MARY) Your tea is as good as it ever was.
(DESMOND *comes into the kitchen.* MIBS *looks at him sullenly*)
MIBS: Who let *you* in?
DESMOND: Your father. He said . . . well, he seems to be in a temper.
MIBS (*Toneless*): That so?
DESMOND: Talk about grumpy: you'd think he was the one with the toothache. (HE *gets no answering smile*) That friend of yours—Dolly Dignam—gave me your message. I was sorry you couldn't come.
MIBS: When? Oh, to the thingummy.
DESMOND: It was lively enough. I don't know if you'd have enjoyed it: there was a rough element. It wasn't quite the occasion they'd hoped for.
MIBS: How was your speech?
DESMOND: Well, I acted the clown, so they laughed a lot. I mean, if they weren't going to take it seriously, why should I? The history professor from Trinity, he got a rough time of it. Still, for the experience—

MIBS: I'm in awful bloody trouble.
DESMOND: —I daresay it was worth it.
MIBS: I said, I'm in—
DESMOND: I know: I heard you. What kind of trouble?
MIBS: Don't ask me.
DESMOND: Is it . . . pyorrhoea?
MIBS: No, it's— Is it what?
DESMOND: She said your father was taking you to the dentist.
MIBS: It was to Father Creedon. (*As* HE *stares at her*) Are you thick? He took me to see old Credo on account of a letter Lar Kearns writ me.
DESMOND: Wrote you. (*Almost laughing*) Lar Kearns?
MIBS: The first letter he ever writ in his flamin' life, and he sends it to me and me da opens it.
DESMOND: It must have been . . . worth reading.
MIBS: You shoulda heard old Credo. (*A florid, booming voice*) "Oh, yass, yass, this is what happens in the house that neglects that grand and glorious Irish custom of the family rosary." Me da was buckin'.
DESMOND: I don't see why.
MIBS (*Sourly*): Do you not!
DESMOND: If Kearns's level of prose is anything like his level of conversation, I can imagine the kind of letter it was. That isn't your fault.
MIBS (*Not answering*): Do you want tea?
DESMOND: If you like.
MIBS: Might as well. I'm to stay here till I'm called. (SHE *sets about making tea*)
DESMOND: Why'd your father open the letter?
MIBS: Because I never get any. 'Specially ones with "S.W.A.L.K." on one side and "S.A.G." on the other. The rotten messer didn't even seal it; he tucked the flap in and put a ha'penny stamp on it.
DESMOND: What did it say?
MIBS: Stuff.
DESMOND: Such as?
MIBS: Things.

DESMOND: Keep it a secret, then.
MIBS: Such a fuss. I went out with a girl I know to Killiney. There was a hop on in the White Cottage, that place on the strand. Lar was at it. He asked me up and bought me a cornet, and at the interval we got two pass-outs and went up on the bank of the railway.
DESMOND: You and he.
MIBS: God, don't you start.
DESMOND: Well?
MIBS: Well nothing. Mind your own business. Anyway, this morning this letter comes. Writ with a pencil, smelling of mackerel, and all slushy and romantic. (*With an embarrassed laugh*) Saying he loved me. I mean, Lar Kearns: would you credit it?
(DESMOND *is silent*)
MIBS (*Continued*): And God, doesn't he put in the lot about him and me on the bank of the railway. You'd think I wasn't there and had to be told. It was like the Grand National on the wireless. He even went and put in extra bits: he must have got them out of some book. When I think of me da reading it: all about me creamy breasts. Two *e*'s in "creamy" and "b-r-e-s-t," "breasts."
DESMOND: Father Creedon must have enjoyed it.
MIBS: Desmond, he was awful, he ate me. I mean, you'd think we'd done something desperate.
DESMOND: I wouldn't know: I wasn't there.
(*The thought of* DESMOND's *being present causes her to giggle*)
DESMOND (*Continued*): Not that I'd want to be.
MIBS (*On the defensive*): We had a coort.
DESMOND: Is that what it's called?
MIBS: Well, blast your nerve.
DESMOND (*Feigning amusement*): A coort!
MIBS: A bit of messin'. I didn't go all the way with him.
DESMOND: Ah-ha.
MIBS: No, I did not.
DESMOND: Wasn't it dark enough?

MIBS: If you want to know, I nearly did. It was the closest I ever came. Only I wouldn't let him. I wouldn't let anyone.
(HE *is unmollified.* SHE *glares at him, fetches the tea tray and slams it down*)
MIBS (*Continued*): Because I haven't the nerve. Here.
DESMOND: I don't want your tea.
MIBS: It's bloody made. (SHE *slushes tea into his cup*) Me da went down to the harbour to see him . . . to see Lar, I mean, and give out to him. (SHE *puts one spoonful of sugar into his cup*) How many?
DESMOND: None.
MIBS: Don't stir it. He says he wants to marry me. (*This is what* SHE *has been leading up to.* SHE *affects to give her attention to putting milk and sugar into her own tea*) I dunno how he came out with it. I bet you me da waved the letter at him and began rantin' and ravin'. And of course you know Lar. If you said you were starvin' he'd tell you seaweed was bread and butter. Whatever he thinks you want to hear, that's what he'll say to you, so I suppose he told me da he'd marry me.
DESMOND: In the letter he said he loved you.
MIBS (*Derisive*): E-eh.
DESMOND: Well, didn't he?
MIBS: Yeah, because he got a red-hot coort . . . don't mind him. So now what am I to do?
DESMOND: Marry him.
MIBS: Ah, for God's sake.
DESMOND: Why not?
MIBS: Old jealous-boots.
DESMOND: Who?
MIBS: He hasn't even a proper job. Give over.
DESMOND: Jobs aren't important. I think you should marry him because I think you're his sort.
MIBS: Yeah, the perfect—(*Her smile dies away as the insult goes home*)
DESMOND: And you won't need a railway bank then, will you, or to be afraid of going all the way with him.

MIBS: Ah, Desmond—
DESMOND: No, you could do worse. I doubt if you'll do better. And you'll be much more your own self at his level than at . . . anyone else's.
(SHE *realises that* HE *is determined to tear down their relationship past all chance of repair*)
MIBS: Sure. Go on, now: go home.
DESMOND: Mm, it's all hours. I'm sure you'll have a happy life. You'll make a nice home for him, perhaps in one of those cottages in the Alley Lane. He needs someone like you: you can help him count his dole money.
MIBS (*Waiting for him to go*): Yeah, thanks.
DESMOND: Because—
MIBS: I said, go. You done what you wanted: you said what can't be took back.
DESMOND: Taken back. (HE *is unable to leave ill enough alone.* HE *wants to draw blood, needs to be certain that her hurt equals his own*) I'm very stupid. I mistook you for someone with self-respect. It was my fault. I thought that at least your ambitions went higher than Lar Kearns.
MIBS: Do you mean you?
DESMOND: I was wrong.
MIBS: Yes . . . you do. Well at least Lar is a bit of gas. I can laugh with him. He's glad of me the way I am. I don't need to have a scaffolding put around me brain before I'm fit to be seen with him. He can give a body a coort and a kiss, and they know it's a person, not bones and cold skin. You think you're so great. Just because you get up and make a speech and they slap you on the back and cheer you, you act like you were someone. Well, you're not. They laugh at you. You have a smell of yourself and you're no one. Honestly, you're not all there, you know that? The whole town knows about the Drumms. Ask them. Go and ask. You're as cracked as your oul' fella was. I'm not surprised he went and—(SHE *breaks off*)
DESMOND: That he what?

MIBS: Go on home.
DESMOND: Yes. (*As* HE *turns to go, the lights fade in the kitchen and come up in the living room.* DRUMM *is in a genial mood*)
DRUMM: It was in that field across from what they called the rabbit wood.
MARY: The back meadow.
DOLLY: There are bungalows now.
MARY: Oh, but then it was the meadow.
DOLLY: Oh, then!
DRUMM: We were walking, the four of us.
KEARNS: Was I there?
DRUMM: My dear man, was Hamlet in Denmark? This, mind you, was in the far-off days when young people wore shabby clothes from poverty rather than affectation. There were still fields to walk in: it was before the country became one vast builder's yard.
MARY: Tell the story.
DRUMM: There were the four of us . . .
DOLLY: The times we had.
DRUMM: And on the path alongside the wood we found a baby bird.
MARY: He's romancin'.
DRUMM: It had fallen from its nest. And he (*Indicating* KEARNS) picked it up.
KEARNS: God bless your memory.
DRUMM: And there in a hedgerow he saw a nest filled with baby birds. So he took this . . . foundling and very tenderly put it in with them.
DOLLY: Ah.
MARY: Well, I'll say this much for him: that's Lar. Now that's him to a T.
KEARNS: Yes, that'd be me.
DRUMM (*To* MARY): I agree with you. It sums him up. Because I went back a week later, and all the other birds had gone. (*To* KEARNS) But yours was still there. Plump and thriving, and no wonder. It was a cuckoo.

MARY: No.
DOLLY: Lar, you didn't.
KEARNS: He's drunk: don't mind him.
MARY: A cuckoo. Oh, that's him, that's the price of him.
   (DRUMM *laughs.* DOLLY *joins in*)
DRUMM: That man . . . put a predator into a—
KEARNS: Yis, more power. Laugh away, make me out a gobshite.
MARY (*Reprimanding him*): Lar.
KEARNS: Take his part, why don't you?
DRUMM: It did happen.
KEARNS: When?
DRUMM: That Sunday.
KEARNS (*Suddenly violent*): In me hump it happened.
MARY: Now, boys, boys . . .
KEARNS: You think I wouldn't recognize a coo-coo? With what I know? Who was it owned Mary Mine?
DRUMM (*Mystified, looking at* MARY): Mary M—
MARY: Not me: his pigeon.
KEARNS: Dezzie, we're all goin' downhill. 'S a fact. And in your case the cells of the brain is handin' in its cards.
DRUMM: Drivel.
KEARNS: Take this evenin'. What did happen, you can't remember, and what didn't happen you have off be heart.
MARY: Can't you take a joke?
DRUMM (*To* MARY): You miss the point.
MARY: No matter: leave it. Dolly, more tea . . .
DRUMM: This afternoon, I took it into my head to go over some old accounts. (*The remark is intended for* MARY) A few figures to be totted up, interest paid, a balance struck.
MARY: Doing sums in this weather.
DRUMM: I sat in the garden. I dragged the deck chair around with me, to keep out of the shadow.
DOLLY: It's still the month of May. Out of the sun it's bitter.
   (DRUMM *looks at her*)

DOLLY (*Continued*): Sorry, love.
KEARNS: The news first, Dolly, then the weather. (HE *laughs*.
DOLLY, *smiling, puts a finger to his lips*)
KEARNS (*Continued*): Ah, God. Say what you like, I'm a great character.
MARY (*To* DRUMM, *prompting*): And then what?
DRUMM: It's no matter.
MARY: Yes, it is. You thought of that day and the four of us.
DRUMM: That unimportant walk we had. From forty years ago: why? What value had it? So I went back to my accounts, and I remembered another time: when a priest came to my aunt's house. I'd been sent to live with her: it was the day of the inquest. He told me to be a brave boy and never turn from God, and he asked a strange question. Had my father written me a letter? I said no: never. I had lived with him in the master's house: why should he write to me? That priest with the pink hand that shook mine: today I remembered him and understood what he'd been after. It was for evidence of suicide . . . the business of burial in consecrated ground.
KEARNS: Suicide? Who?
MARY: Priest and all, the cheek of him.
DOLLY: Aren't people dreadful?
DRUMM: Why?
MARY: Why? Being killed like your da was is one thing, but to take the poor man's character . . .
DRUMM: How?
KEARNS: I remember him: a decent skin. He taught me.
DRUMM: Now *that's* taking his character. (*To* MARY) And if the poor man, as you call him, did die by accident, it was by the same law of probability as being run down by the Dun Laoghaire mailboat halfway up the Volga.
MARY: Desmond, you have no nature in you.
DOLLY: Honestly and truly, some people have nothing better to do than spread stories.
KEARNS: It was a mishap. He was shortcuttin' it through the tunnel.
DRUMM: That was the coroner's finding.

KEARNS: Down the bank at the Ramparts, through the dark along the railway line and up the bank again. I done it meself.
DRUMM: Boys do it, yes.
KEARNS: Oh, a dangerous pastime.
DRUMM: At school I was informed with some glee that he had put his head on the track.
MARY: You're not to say that.
DRUMM: The town says it.
MARY: When? I never heard it.
KEARNS: No, nor I.
DRUMM (*To* MARY): I thought you did.
(*Almost certainly,* MARY *has forgotten their old quarrel, but* SHE *senses an accusation*)
MARY: You were wrong, then. And your song and dance about it has Dolly upset.
DRUMM (*To* DOLLY): Are you? Why?
DOLLY: It was the thought of a soul going to hell.
DRUMM: My father?
DOLLY: It's what the Church says. A mortal sin.
DRUMM: I know what the Church says. That the creator of heaven and earth is a bungler who burns his mistakes. Tommyrot. God made him, let God put up with him. At least He knew him; I never did. Whatever was breakable in him, he kept under lock and key, away from vandals. Sooner a shuttered house than a plundered one. You were welcome to what was left, what passed for all there was of him . . . the bones and cold skin. If he ever tried to speak to me, or to anyone, it was in that tunnel. And damn them: they called it an accident, so he said nothing. (*To* MARY) I'd say that was taking his character. (*A pause.* HE *looks at his watch; then with a social smile*) Well, now.
DOLLY (*Taking her cue*): It was gorgeous.
MARY: Where are you harin' off to?
KEARNS: They're not goin'. (*To* DRUMM) Will you sit?
DRUMM: Tomorrow is Monday. I'm not on a perpetual holiday, like some. (*Not unkindly*) Do you know, this man's

continued survival without ever lifting a finger makes the mystery of the Holy Trinity look like a card trick.
DOLLY (*Laughing*): Poor Lar.
KEARNS: You'll have a tincture.
DRUMM: I will not.
KEARNS: To see yous up the hill. I've two jars left for meself, and if yous go home on me she'll have them locked up before you're on Sorrento Road. You will.
MARY: Humour him.
DRUMM: One, and that's all. (*To* DOLLY) Yes?
DOLLY: I'm enjoying myself. And you are, too: don't pretend. Dezzie got great news this morning.
KEARNS: That a fact?
DRUMM (*Muted*): Dolly . . .
DOLLY (*Winking at* MARY): It's a secret.
KEARNS (*Getting the drinks*): Ah, but Dezzie, the changes in this town. If your da, God be good to him, cem back again, he wouldn't know a bit of it.
DRUMM: I'm sure.
KEARNS: He would not. If you told him the oul' steam trains was gone, he wouldn't believe you.
(THEY *stare at him.* HE *realises his gaffe and makes a bumbling attempt to cover up*)
KEARNS (*Continued*): An' . . . an' the poor oul' trams, wha'? Yis. An' . . . an' the fizz-bags the chiselurs could buy for a ha'penny. An' did j'ever go out in the Sound and look at the nuns on the rocks below the Loreto, with the striped bathin' togs down to their ankles?
DRUMM: You've drained life's cup to the full, haven't you?
MARY (*Smiling*): Trust him!
(*To* KEARNS, *privately,* SHE *presents a bunched fist for his indiscretion about the trains*)
KEARNS: Yis. An' do you 'member Cussin's shop? With the yoke for slicin' the rashers. I'd stand for hours and look at that thing goin' round. It was better than the pictures.
MARY: Give the man his drink.
KEARNS: True as God. Zz . . . zzz . . .

DOLLY: Did it have a happy ending? (SHE *almost blushes at her own daring.* DRUMM *is surprised, almost admiring*)
DRUMM: Well, now.
KEARNS: Did it have what?
MARY: Was Laurel and Hardy in it?
(*There is a faint yelp from* DOLLY. KEARNS *ignores her*)
KEARNS: And, Dezzie, I'll tell you what else I remember. Girls, will yous listen. A bit o' shush. No, this is as true as God. (*Impressively*) An' it was the best thing that ever happened to me.
(DOLLY *mutters inaudibly*)
DRUMM: I can't hear you. (*As* SHE *shakes her head*) Say it and don't mumble.
DOLLY: *Gone With the Wind* was on the bacon slicer. (*Her laughter goes out of control.* MARY *joins in*)
DRUMM: Dear God.
MARY: Desmond, will you stop her?
DRUMM: Dolly, that will do. I said, it's quite enough. (*His voice trembles.* HE *leans his head on one hand*)
KEARNS (*Still trying*): No, as true as you're sitting. In the whole o' me life, the best thing that ever—Well, if yous are all goin' to make a shaggin' heehaw of it—
MARY: We're listening.
(*A whimper from* DOLLY. DRUMM *nudges her and, unwilling to trust himself to speak, signals to* KEARNS *to continue*)
KEARNS: There was nothing like it before nor since.
MARY: This'll be good.
DRUMM: You might get a compliment.
MARY: Not before its time.
KEARNS: I'll tell yous . . .
MARY: Do.
KEARNS: It was the day Workman won the National.
MARY: Thanks very much.
DOLLY (*A handkerchief to her mouth*): Mmm . . .
KEARNS: Yous can laugh. It was the time herself and me were as poor as Job's ass. Nothin' comin' in only a few

shillin's assistance, and your one here expectin'. Weren't you? You were expectin' Sean.
MARY (*A hint of reserve*): I might have been.
KEARNS: No one remembers nothin' tonight. Yes, you were, and your da was six months dead, so he couldn't help us. Yis, hard times. Herself had a path worn between here and the pawn office. Everythin' you could wrap up in a parcel, so's it wouldn't shame you. The watch her da left her: thirty years on the trams. An' there was this sweepstake up in Larkin's-that-was, a draw on the National. I won a couple o' bob that day playin' pitch-an'-toss, so I said to meself: "I'll risk the lot." An' didn't I draw a horse, and wasn't it Workman?
DRUMM: Highly appropriate.
KEARNS: You're right. Well, I wasn't worth me salt till the day o' the—
(DOLLY, *as a result of* DRUMM's *remark, holds back another fit of laughter and gets to her feet*)
MARY: Dolly, are you all right?
DOLLY: Grand. I'll just use your upstairs. Excuse me.
DRUMM (*Mischievously, as* SHE *passes*): Disgraceful woman.
(SHE *slaps at his shoulder and hurries out. In the passageway,* SHE *releases her laughter in one gasp.* SHE *leans against the wall, recovering. During what follows,* SHE *goes out of sight, presumably upstairs*)
KEARNS: It must be Dolly's night for laughin'. Yis, now where was I . . . ?
DRUMM: Presumably the horse won.
KEARNS: Dezzie, it walked it. Fifty quid put into me fist, and I mean fifty quid then, not now. We were landed.
DRUMM: I'd say so.
KEARNS: Steeped. We were in the clear. Everythin' back from the pawn—may I drop down dead, I had to borry a handcart—and the pram and the stuff for the baby bought and paid for. Dezzie . . .
DRUMM: What?
KEARNS: It was the hand o' God.

DRUMM: Was it?
KEARNS: I said to meself the day the lad was born: "He didn't see us stuck, and I'll never doubt Him be worryin' again."
DRUMM: A promise you kept.
KEARNS: I never reneged.
DRUMM: God will provide.
KEARNS: Leave it to Him.
DRUMM: And He watches over you?
MARY: Over all of us.
KEARNS: Them that has faith in Him.
DRUMM: Ah, yes. Don't dig the garden: pray for an earthquake.
KEARNS: Jeer away.
DRUMM: Faith? If either of us, you or I, had a scrap of it, we'd be in a monastery living on black bread and doing atonement. What we have is hope. We call it faith.
KEARNS: Rubbidge.
DRUMM: Mind, I'll concede that as a race we have more to believe in than others. Christians elsewhere worship three Divine Persons: God the Father, the Son and the Holy Ghost. We have added a fourth one: God the Jockey.
KEARNS: You won't act the hard root when your time comes.
MARY: Now, Lar . . .
KEARNS: Then what'll you do?
DRUMM: Envy you your certainty.
KEARNS (*Crowing*): Ah! You've had it too soft, Dezzie. No goin' short, nothin' to pray for. A grand cushy job with a collar an' tie on it, an' a pension in the windup.
MARY: Don't row with the man.
KEARNS: What rowin'? Sure more power to him. I'm only sayin' that poor people like ourselves, them that has it hard, we're more in with God, like, than the rest of them.
DRUMM: He's one of your own.
KEARNS (*Delighted*): Now you have it. (*Grabbing* DRUMM's *glass*) Gimme that.

DRUMM: I won't.
KEARNS (*Masterful*): I say you will.
DRUMM: A cushy job, you called it. Perhaps it is. But a man who carves penny whistles at least knows his own worth: I don't know mine. If I licked envelopes all day, the pay would be the same. I spend a third of my life in a hot-house of intrigue and skulduggery which would make the court of the Borgias seem like a whist drive, and I do work of doubtful value for a government of doubtful morality. *Cogito ergo sum.* I am a cog, therefore I am.
KEARNS: Still, isn't it money for jam?
DRUMM: Quite.
KEARNS: And you're on the home stretch now, with the pension at the winnin' post.
DRUMM: If God doesn't get there first.
KEARNS: Not forgettin' the lump sum.
DRUMM: True.
KEARNS: Paid for, don't forget, by yours truly.
MARY: By who?
KEARNS: Income tax. I don't begrudge it to you. Only it's time you stopped takin' life so serious. Y'ought to pop off some place: folly the sun. An' give Dolly a bit of a break. That's a great girl.
MARY: He's right there.
KEARNS: A topper.
DRUMM: Yes.
KEARNS: "Yes," says he. Say it an' mean it.
DRUMM: You seem to think that at this late stage in her life she needs references.
KEARNS: I'm sayin' you got the right girl, the same as meself did. Only you were slow in findin' out, on account of you had a soft spot for this one.
MARY: Now no blatherin'.
KEARNS: I don't miss much.
MARY (*Embarrassed*): I'll guzzle him.
KEARNS: What harm's in sayin' it? We're all past that sort o' jack-actin', wha'? The blood is gone cool.

MARY: In a minute it won't be the only thing.
KEARNS: No, own up to it, I wiped your eye. And sign's on it you got Dolly and she's a credit to you.
DRUMM: I'm sure.
KEARNS: *Be* sure.
DRUMM (*Becoming nettled*): Yes, now could we have done?
KEARNS: A smasher, so she is.
DRUMM: My dear man, don't tell me about it: tell Dolly.
KEARNS: I did tell her.
DRUMM: Well, then.
KEARNS: Many's the time.
DRUMM: Well done.
KEARNS: More times than you told her.
DRUMM: No doubt.
KEARNS: In this room you're sittin' in.
MARY (*Anxiously*): Lar . . .
KEARNS: Last Friday.
   (*A pause.* DRUMM *is quite still*)
KEARNS (*Continued*): No. No, it was the time I met her up the town. Yis, that was when I told her.
   (DRUMM *looks at him with contempt*)
MARY: That tongue of yours: it ought to be cut out of you.
KEARNS: Wha's up?
MARY: You'd talk if it killed you. A mouth. A mouth, that's what you are, no good for an'thin' else.
KEARNS: I met her up the town—
MARY: Shut that gob of yours. Shut it. (*To* DRUMM) She came in for a cup of coffee. She'd do her shoppin' and buy the few things for the week, and she'd come and I'd put the kettle on. No harm in that.
   (DRUMM *is silent*)
MARY (*Continued*): Ten minutes the one day in the week. She has her neighbours: who else has she? Do you expect her to live like a statue? I said to her: "Tell him, why can't you?" She said: "I'm afraid to."
   (DRUMM *does not react. A faint cough as* DOLLY *comes into view outside*)

A LIFE Act Two

MARY (*Continued*): (*Hearing her*) Now let it lie. You will.
(DOLLY *comes in*)
DOLLY: Honestly and truly, I'm weak from laughing. Look at me: I'm a sight for the crows.
(DRUMM *looks towards her*)
DOLLY (*Continued*): You're very quiet. Is something up? (*Touching her hair*) Is it me?
(*The lights cross-fade with those in the kitchen.* DESMOND *is standing facing* MIBS *and* LAR. HE *is holding a package.* LAR *is wearing a new off-the-peg blue serge suit*)
DESMOND: I'm sorry. I came to leave a message. Your father said I was to come in.
LAR: Cough-Bottle, the hard man: I wouldn't know a bit o' you. Hey, c'm'ere an' tell us. (*Modelling the suit*) Is this the berries or isn't it?
DESMOND: Pardon me?
LAR: The suit. I was tryin' it on for Mibs.
DESMOND: Very smart.
LAR: It's new. You're supposed to say "Well wear."
DESMOND: Well wear.
LAR: Might as well go to me doom in style, wha'? Fifty-two an' a tanner . . . five bob a week.
MIBS: Don't tell everyone our business. (*To* DESMOND, *coldly*) Did you want something?
DESMOND: I was at the Sodality Mass yesterday. I heard the banns being read out . . .
MIBS (*Flatly*): Did you?
DESMOND: It was the first I knew of it.
LAR (*Revelling in his moment*): Wasn't it lovely? . . . Makin' a show of a man, readin' his names out from altar. Dezzie, she landed me. Talk about a conger eel: you never seen the fight I put up, an' just when I was away an' clear with the hook in me mouth, she stuck the gaff into me.
MIBS: Dry up.
LAR: The banns called, the new suit bought and the chapel

booked. Here, look at the way I'm shanghaied. (*Taking hold of* MIBS's *left hand*) Show him.
(SHE *pulls her hand away*)
LAR (*Continued*): The diamond cem out of a watch.
DESMOND: Anyway, I thought I'd offer my congratulations.
MIBS: Thanks.
LAR: Me oul' comrade, put it there.
DESMOND (*Offering the package*): This isn't very much. Just to . . . mark the occasion.
LAR: Ah, for the love-a! (*Feeling the shape*) It's a book.
DESMOND: Nearly as bad. But with every good wish.
LAR: Can we open it?
DESMOND: Well, it's not for Christmas. (*Less abrasively*) Of course. (*To* MIBS) When is the . . . uh?
MIBS: The second.
DESMOND: Ah.
LAR: Did you hear tell her da put me to work? 'S a fact. He found me a spiffin' job. I'm in it for life.
DESMOND: Oh, yes?
LAR: I'm on the trams.
DESMOND: Good for you. As a conductor?
LAR (*Shaking his head*): I'm above in the yard. Not so much on them as under them. Sure isn't it a start? Hold on: I have it. (HE *has undone the wrapping and finds an attractively framed Van Gogh print. It is a still-life: "Yellow Chair with Pipe." We have already seen this reproduction; it is hanging in the living room*)
LAR (*Continued*): (*To* MIBS) It's a pitcher.
DESMOND: Not the original, I'm afraid. It's by Van Gogh, a Dutch artist. I've always been fond of it.
LAR: Mibs, have a dekko.
(SHE *moves reluctantly to inspect it*)
DESMOND: Wherever it is you'll be living, I thought you might find a place for it.
LAR: Mibs's oul' lad: he says we can bunk here.
DESMOND: I see.
LAR: Until we find a place. Dezzie, about the weddin'. The

spondulicks is a bit short, so there'll only be her parents an' me ma, an' Harry Young, that's standin' up for me.
DESMOND: I understand.
LAR: I mean, don't expect a card in the post with gold writin' on it. You have me?
DESMOND (*Heartily*): Yes!
LAR: You're sure now?
MIBS (*Suddenly*): It's only an old chair.
DESMOND: That's all.
MIBS: A bit of wood standing there; it's nothing. But it's like as if whoever done it . . . got himself inside of it. (SHE *smiles at* DESMOND, *delighted by her discovery*)
LAR: Give us a gawk. Hey, it's crooked. I wouldn't sit on that yoke. (*Remembering his manners*) It's nice an' bright, but. Great in a room.
(*It is the difference between the two reactions that provokes* DESMOND *into the following*)
DESMOND: Mary, if I might talk to you . . .
MIBS: Talk away.
DESMOND: No . . . un . . . (HE *indicates* LAR)
MIBS: If you mean where he can't hear us, no, you can't.
DESMOND (*To* LAR): You don't mind.
MIBS: Yes, he does. (*To* LAR) Stay where you are. (*To* DESMOND) I know what you want to say, and I'll save you the trouble. "Marry Lar," you told me, "you're his sort." And you were right.
DESMOND: No.
LAR: Decent man. Won't forget it to you.
MIBS: Yes, you were. You used to say to me: "Think for yourself." Many's a time you said it. "Put this on one side and that on the other and look at them." And it's what I done. (*Amending*) What I did. And I knew that with Lar there'd be a bit of me left over. Not with you: you'd want the lot. The bit of me that's not yours at all: that likes to go to a do or a hop and sing songs on the road home. Or talk too loud and say "Shag it" and be what you call common. You'd take it all: there'd be nothing left for Lar, not even the bit of harmless likin'.

You don't know where halfway is. Lar does: he's glad of what you can give him. He won't begrudge you the bit of me that's yours. (*With a grin*) Even though you'll turn your nose up at it.
(*A pause.* LAR *has been listening with an amiable, uncomprehending smile.* DESMOND, *knowing his cause is lost, wants to back out with at least his pride intact*)
DESMOND: I don't take leavings.
MIBS: Hard lines, then.
DESMOND: Yes . . . well, you know best. (*Formally*) I'm obliged to you for the courtesy of a—
MIBS: Oh, balls.
DESMOND (*Ignoring this*): And forgive the intrusion. I wanted to wish you both all . . . (*Unable to resist the inflection*) possible happiness.
LAR: Look, sit down.
MIBS: Let him alone.
LAR: Well, listen . . . you're to drop in on us, do you hear? No makin' strange.
MIBS: And thanks for the picture.
DESMOND: Oh . . . there's a card with it. The very best, then.
MIBS: Yeah. 'Bye, now.
(HE *goes.* LAR *follows him to the door*)
LAR (*Calling*): Now if you don't drop in you'll be back o' the neck: I mean it. Hey . . . and don't pick up any good things. (HE *comes back into the room.* MIBS *is searching the wrapping paper and finds a greetings card*)
LAR (*Continued*): I think the Cough-Bottle's gettin' a bit queer in himself, do you not? Too much oul' readin' an' stuff. (HE *looks at the picture*) Hey, was I polite to him?
MIBS: You were great. Change out of that suit.
LAR: 'Cause I wouldn't like to hurt his feelin's. Whoever sold him that yoke rooked him.
(MIBS *is reading, half-audibly*)
LAR (*Continued*): What's on it?
MIBS: "For there is good news yet to hear and fine things to be seen, Before we go to Paradise by way of Ken . . . sal Green."

LAR: Wha's it mean?
MIBS: Nothing. It doesn't mean anything. Except that he'd make me finish that bloody lesson if it killed him.
(*The lights cross-fade with those in the living area.* DOLLY *is tense and silent.* MARY *is trying to keep up the pretence that the evening is on the same relaxed level as previously*)
MARY (*Referring to* KEARNS): One day he was off out mowin' her grass, and the next he was puttin' a washer on her tap, and the day after that her roof needed mendin'.
KEARNS (*Protesting*): Now you're makin' a yarn of it.
MARY: "A poor widow," says me man here, "with no one to do her a hand's turn." Oh aye, I thought to myself, that's how it starts. Josie Murnaghan on the Barrack Road . . . Josie McDonald that was. (*To* DOLLY) You know her.
(DOLLY *shakes her head*)
MARY (*Continued*): Ah, you do. Well, 'clare to God, I was at the state where I was examinin' his coat for hairs.
KEARNS: Yis, at my age.
MARY: The older they are, the worse they are. Next thing, he says her wall needs whitewashin'. "It's a big job," says he. "I know," says I, "I've seen her." And then, doesn't this woman, a total stranger, come to the door, and a little boy with her, and he roarin'. Him . . . (*Meaning* KEARNS) it turns out he's after burstin' the child's chestnut. He was never next or near Josie Murnaghan; he was off playin' . . . (*To* KEARNS) What?
KEARNS: Conkers.
MARY: Conkers . . . with the little chiselers off the road.
DOLLY (*Faintly; a glance at* DRUMM): Goodness.
MARY: When he ought to be sayin' his prayers.
DOLLY: Oh, now.
MARY: A right go-be-the-wall. But sure there wasn't a family yet where there weren't secrets.
KEARNS: She thought I was—
MARY (*Silencing him; to* DRUMM): Do you hear me?
DRUMM: Perfectly.

MARY: So will you come out of your sulks.
DRUMM (*Not harshly*): Now don't interfere.
MARY: You can blame it on me. I met her in McLoughlin's one day, and I said: "Come back to the house." She didn't want to. I made her.
DRUMM: At gunpoint.
MARY: What?
DRUMM: You abducted her.
MARY: No, I didn't need to. But Desmond, don't go gettin' sarky with me, not in here. This is my house you're sittin' in.
DRUMM: That can be rectified.
MARY: It can, yes, and off you go again. But for how long this time?
(*It is a reminder.* HE *looks at her resentfully*)
MARY (*Continued*): That'd suit you. You could spend the rest of your life with your feelings hurt: being cool with one half o' the world and not talking to the other half.
DOLLY (*Not wanting a scene*): Don't . . .
KEARNS: I think we ought to be all grand and sociable and as happy as Larry. I wasn't christened be accident, you know.
MARY: Have sense. What did she do on you? Nothin'.
DRUMM: Whatever Dolly did or did not do, I don't wish to discuss it outside my own home.
KEARNS: Proper order.
MARY: You hold your tongue. (*To* DRUMM) Too true you don't. Because you know I'm well able for you and she isn't. She walks on tippytoes around you. When you come home like a divil because someone has got on the wrong side of you, she has to put up with it. I don't.
DRUMM: I agree. And you won't have to. Dolly . . .
MARY: No. You'll go out of here when you tell that woman she done nothing wrong. Ah, Desmond: all this because she was still talking to me when you were black out with us.
DRUMM (*Indignantly*): No.
MARY: What, then?

DRUMM: Nothing of the sort. Dolly is free to make friends. Or to lose them, or keep them: it's her choice. I don't ask her to live in my pocket. I don't want it.
MARY: Then for the love an' honour—
DRUMM: Because of the deception. How do you think it feels to know that one has been listening to the same lie for five years?
DOLLY (*Timidly; helpfully*): Six.
(HE *looks at her as if suspecting an attempt at humour. Then*)
DRUMM: Six.
MARY: I know, yes. And all the harm it did you!
DRUMM: It was behind my back. You knew and he knew. Probably half the town did as well.
MARY: Now we have it. The town.
DRUMM: And laughed at me for a fool.
MARY: Oh, aye: the town. What'll the town say?
DRUMM: I don't give a damn what it says, but I will not stand arraigned before a judge and jury of gossipmongers and idlers.
MARY: You're so fond of yourself.
DRUMM: They had their day.
MARY: You told us. They made a mock of you because you were out of step, so you got your own back on them. You stopped walkin'. You were going to do the divil an' all: yes, you were . . . but no, you might get laughed at. You let on they're not worth passing the time of day with, but they rule you.
DOLLY: Mary, they do not.
DRUMM: Thank you, I can defend myself.
MARY: It's true: they bett you.
DRUMM: Beat me.
MARY: However you say it.
DRUMM: I fear them, yes. I fear their easy freemasonry. But if I failed to do what you call the devil and all, it wasn't on their account. It was because the devil and all wasn't in me. But I'll tell you what is. I've never lied to or about a

man. I've never smiled into the face of a knave, or pretended to see virtue where I found none. Or been a loafer or a hanger-on, or licked a boot. I don't call that a total defeat. I grant you there's a debit side to those accounts. Too much pride, too little charity. And if it makes you happy, the reason I was angry with Dolly is that I can no longer afford to be angry with her. I consider that . . . an imposition.

(MARY's *smile is hard as* SHE *turns to* DOLLY. *Inside her, probably to her own surprise, an old wound has been reopened*)

MARY (*To* DOLLY): There, now. Isn't he good to you?

KEARNS: That's the dart: forgive an' forget. Sure who could be cross with Dolly? And Dezzie is not the worst o' them either.

MARY: Oh, he's a great man.

(DRUMM *catches the note of hostility.* HE *looks at her, puzzled*)

DOLLY: I'm glad Dezzie found out.

KEARNS: A fuss over nothin'.

DOLLY: Because I hate anything that's hole-and-corner. (*To* MARY) I do, I told you.

DRUMM: It's over and done with.

MARY (*To* DOLLY): It is. Everything except the absolution and the three Hail Marys.

DRUMM (*To* DOLLY): We must go. (*To* MARY) You're in a fighting mood.

MARY: Am I?

KEARNS (*To* MARY): But be the holy, you're a fierce woman. Goin' for him bald-headed, wha'?

DRUMM: Mary herself says it: she's well able for me. (*To* DOLLY) Had you a coat?

KEARNS: Still, there's one thing that's askin' for a puck in the gob, an' that's to go interferin' between a man an' a wife. I thought he was goin' to draw out at you.

DRUMM: It was close. If today hadn't been Sunday . . . !

(DOLLY *laughs*)

KEARNS (*To* MARY): Thre was a narra escape for you.
MARY: He interfered between *us*.
   (*The suddenness of the accusation takes* DRUMM *off guard*)
KEARNS (*Unheeding*): Oh, a comical card.
DRUMM: Do you mean me?
MARY: So exchange is no robbery.
DRUMM: Interfered between you? I never did.
KEARNS: Between *us?* Begod, he'd have his work cut out for him, so he would. What are you carryin' on about?
DRUMM: How did I? Well?
   (SHE *retreats from the edge. Her manner becomes sullen, evasive*)
MARY: Coming in here, telling us how great you are. Never told a lie in your life, never kowtowed to anyone, never done nothin'. A saint, so you are. And poor oul' Dolly, the row there was over a mangy cup of coffee in her hand the one day in the week.
DRUMM: I thought that was settled.
KEARNS: Don't mind her.
DRUMM: You said I interfered between the two of you.
KEARNS: Not at all. She's romancin'.
DRUMM: I'm asking her what she meant.
MARY: Nothing.
DOLLY: Dezzie, leave it. She's upset.
DRUMM (*Gently*): Mary? Are you going to tell me?
   (SHE *shakes her head*)
DRUMM (*Continued*): No need, then? Are we friends?
MARY (*Almost in despair*): Yes.
KEARNS: Certainly we're friends. Who the hell says different?
DRUMM: That's what matters. We'll see you soon. (HE *has taken* MARY's *hand.* SHE *keeps a grip on his when* HE *makes to leave*)
MARY: This morning . . . you said about what you were owed. I've no head for words . . . credit and something.
DRUMM: Debit and credit.
MARY: To add up with.

DRUMM: To add and subtract.
MARY: I thought all day about it. At first I said No, then I said: "It's what's due to him." And that's why. Not to harm you . . . I wouldn't, but you have the right. (*A pause*) You were good to Sean. No one could have—
KEARNS (*In alarm*): Eh . . . eh . . .
MARY: —could have done more for him. You paid for him at the Christian Brothers, you taught him, made a scholar of him . . .
KEARNS (*Thundering*): And I say you won't!
MARY: You took him for walks with you. Yourself and Dolly and the girls, yous brung him with yous that time for a holiday. The day of his confirmation, you put the suit on his back. It was "Uncle Desmond, Uncle Desmond" . . . all we ever heard out of him. Now I'm not saying you meant to do it—
KEARNS: I'm boss here, and I'm tellin' you "No."
MARY: I'm not saying that. But you turned him against Lar.
KEARNS (*At* DRUMM *and* DOLLY): *Get out, get out.*
DRUMM: No. Untrue.
MARY: Maybe without meaning to . . .
DRUMM: It is untrue.
MARY: His father was good-for-nothing. He was lazy. He was useless. He smelled of porter. He was ignorant.
KEARNS (*Weakly*): I told you. The lad an' me . . . ile an' water.
DRUMM: This is not true.
MARY: You never said a word against Lar: I'll give you that. But you schooled him well: he heard you talk to Lar and he seen you look at him. Sean couldn't be in the same room with him. Do you wonder he got the idea into his head?
KEARNS: She's tellin' lies.
DRUMM: Say it then. This . . . idea.
MARY: He said it to us. The time he had the row with Lar and went off to England. It's why you've heard the last of him. The exam he passed that summer and the marks

they gave him. Maybe he wondered where he got his brains from.

(DRUMM *and* MARY *look at each other. A pause*)

KEARNS: Dezzie, listen—

MARY: Be quiet now.

KEARNS: —a bee in his bonnet.

MARY (*Ignoring him, to* DRUMM): So now you can do your adding up.

DRUMM: The boy left here because he—

KEARNS: Not at all. (*To* MARY) All them years gone by, dead an' buried. What the hell did you want to go upsettin' the man for?

MARY: It wasn't to harm him.

DRUMM: I don't accept it. Very well: I took too much upon myself. He was your son: I meddled, I went where I had no business to go. I'd go there again, because it was to find him a place in the world, away from street corners. He was a fine boy: worthwhile . . . he had manners. I cared for him. But to put that idea into his head, to work that kind of mischief; no. Not I.

DOLLY: Dezzie wouldn't, Mary. It's not in him.

DRUMM (*Looking at* MARY): Even without meaning to.

KEARNS: Sure don't we know, aren't we sayin'? Me oul' comrade, wha'?

DRUMM (*To* KEARNS): And you. You've known why the boy went, what he believed, and all these years you've made me welcome in this house.

KEARNS: Why wouldn't I? Aren't we pals, tried an' true, the last o' the oul' stock. Put it there!

(DRUMM *accepts his hand*)

DRUMM (*It is the nearest* HE *has come to liking* KEARNS): You really are an impossible man.

KEARNS: An' in the heel o' the hunt wasn't it tit for tat? I took your one here offa you. So you took the lad, and aren't we even?

(DRUMM *looks at him in shock. It is as if a blow had been struck*)

KEARNS (*Continued*): Listen, you'll have a jar. There's a drop still in the—
(DRUMM *turns and goes out.* DOLLY *starts after him, sees his raincoat, picks it up and follows him. The lights dim on the living room and come up on the bandstand.* DESMOND, MIBS, LAR *and* DOROTHY *are there.* THEY *watch as* DRUMM *comes into view.* HE *stops, as if from exhaustion*)

LAR: We'll scram off outa here to some place else. Are yous on?

DOROTHY: I know . . . we'll go to the White Rock.

MIBS: That'll take us till all hours. I have a tea to get ready.

LAR: Tell yous what. We'll go up Higgins's Hill and 'round be the Back Meadow. I'll show yous a bird's nest. Hey, Cough-Bottle . . . mind the missus for me. (LAR *takes* DOROTHY *by the hand.* MIBS *follows.* DESMOND *looks at* DRUMM *and is the last to go.* DOLLY *appears*)

DOLLY: Honestly and truly, going off without your coat. You're asking for it. Are you all right?

DRUMM: I walked too fast. Give me a moment.

DOLLY: Put this on.

DRUMM: Yes.

DOLLY: I mean now. (SHE *helps him into his coat*) What Mary said, you're never taking it to heart? Such a thing for her to come out with.

DRUMM: Wasn't it!

DOLLY: And poor Lar . . . you'd pity him.

DRUMM: One day . . .

DOLLY: What, love?

DRUMM: I'll take a microscope and an axe. With the microscope I'll discover where his brain is, and then I'll sink the axe into it.

DOLLY: Will you stop . . . no one minds you.

DRUMM: I know.

DOLLY: I think Mary has a jealous streak in her. The way she's forever trying to make out that you and she are so great. It's to show off in front of me.

DRUMM: Dolly...
DOLLY: I mean, she missed her chance. You were the brainiest boy in the town, and now it's too late. Lord knows I'm fond of her, but it's her own fault. (SHE *sees that* DRUMM *is glaring at her*) I'm listening, pet.
DRUMM: I've achieved nothing.
DOLLY: How?
DRUMM: Three hundred days a year for forty years... I've spent twelve thousand days doing work I despise. Instead of friends, I've had standards, and woe betide those who failed to come up to them. Well, *I* failed. My contempt for the town, for the wink and the easy nod and the easier grin... it was cowardice: Mary was right. What I called principles was vanity. What I called friendship was malice.
DOLLY: Will you go 'way. This is because Mary upset you.
DRUMM: Not much to boast of at the end of the day.
DOLLY: The end, how are you.
DRUMM: Well, is it?
DOLLY: You're in the glooms: I'm not going to answer you. And if it was true itself...
DRUMM: Well?
DOLLY: And it isn't, not a blessed word of it. You have me as bad as yourself.
DRUMM: Go on. If it were true itself...
DOLLY: I was going to say, if it *was* true, it needn't be from now on. I mean, Dezzie, are we alive or aren't we? (*Pause*) Now don't stand here: come home. Look at the way the evenings are getting a stretch: there's still light in the sky.
DRUMM: I have a question.
DOLLY (*Smiling*): More silliness.
DRUMM: Supposing I were to offer you a choice between buying a motorcar—
DOLLY (*Excited*): Dezzie!
DRUMM: Be quiet. Between that and my writing a book about this place. Which would you choose?
DOLLY (*After a pause*): The motorcar.

DRUMM (*A little sadly*): Of course you would.
DOLLY: Because . . . whatever I want, you do the opposite.
DRUMM: You are a most aggravating woman: you get more foolish every day. Go . . . be off home with you. Make a start.

(THEY *set off*)

CURTAIN

A Life is the second play by Hugh Leonard to be produced on Broadway. His first, *"Da,"* won the Tony, New York Critics' Circle, Drama Desk and Outer Critics' Circle awards for Best Play 1978. Mr. Leonard was born in Dublin in 1926. He has written more than twenty stage plays, all of which have been performed either in Dublin or London. They include *The Patrick Pearse Motel, Madigan's Lock, Some of My Best Friends Are Husbands, Mick and Mick, Thieves,* and *A Suburb of Babylon*. In addition, *The Au Pair Man, Stephen D, Summer,* and *The Poker Session* have all been performed in New York. Mr. Leonard has written extensively for television in England, with many original plays as well as serializations and adaptations of Dickens, Emily Brontë, Flaubert, Maugham, Wilkie Collins, Conan Doyle, Maupassant, James Joyce and Sean O'Faoláin. His films include *Interlude, Great Catherine* and *Rake's Progress*. He lives with his wife, Paule, and daughter, Danielle, not far from Dublin. His interests are: friends, spying on passing ships through a telescope, travel, chess, and strong drink. He is always glad to visit the U.S., as he considers it the only part of the world that hasn't become Americanized.